LOGIC
and
PROOF

LOGIC and PROOF

Marvin L. Bittinger
Indiana University

ADDISON-WESLEY PUBLISHING COMPANY
Reading, Massachusetts • Menlo Park, California • London • Don Mills, Ontario

Reproduced by Addison-Wesley from camera-ready copy prepared by the author.

To

Nelson L. Zinsmeister

PREFACE

The purpose of this text is to provide a basic background in symbolic logic which is connected to mathematical proofs and attainable at an early level in the undergraduate curriculum.

There are various uses to which the book is addressed. The author has effectively used this material both as a supplement to the last semester of calculus, with an extra hour of credit given upon completion, as well as an introduction to a junior level course on the real number system. It was found that both greatly speeded later study for the student knew how to form sentence negations, commence proofs by contradiction, commence proofs by mathematical induction, and so on. The text could also be used as a supplement to existing, or nonexisting, logic sections in algrebra and analysis texts.

Exercise sets are of two types: longer sets that occur at the end of sections, and smaller sets which occur within the written material allowing the student to get more involved in the discussion by asking him to complete a development or proof. For convenience, answers immediately follow exercise sets. There are also two diagnostic tests.

The section on set theory in Chapter 1 could effectively be skipped, apart from notation, by those with prior background.

The author wishes to express his appreciation to a number of people. Professor Angelo Margaris of The Ohio State University whose teaching of a short unit in logic aided a group of struggling students and provided the bud of the idea to the author. Conversations with Professor M. L. Keedy of Purdue University were both helpful and inspiring. The typing of Mrs. Peter Leeds was splendid.

M. L. B.

Indianapolis, Indiana
1970

TABLE OF CONTENTS

INTRODUCTION

Just as an artist uses various tools and styles in his work, so does the mathematician. The purpose of this text is to study logic and to connect this to mathematical proofs; the tools of the mathematician.

A person can study impressionism, expressionism and so on, can know all about water colors, oils and canvas; but never be an artist. However, such knowledge does provide a firmer foundation for being an artist. Similarly, your study of this material does not guarantee you will be able to prove all you encounter, but should enhance your ability to do mathematical proofs.

When you reach an exercise set cover the answers with a piece of paper or card. Then write out the answers in the blanks, if provided, or on a separate sheet of paper. Below the exercises are the answers. Compare your answers with the given ones. If you get stuck on an exercise, use the answers for hints, but avoid the usual crutch of turning to the answers without a thorough effort. When you are asked to give a proof, keep in mind that more than one way is possible and compare your proof to the given one.

You will have two examinations to help evaluate how well you have learned the material.

As you study more advanced mathematics the importance of learning (memorizing) definitions cannot be overemphasized. Keep a notebook and write definitions down. Material will be provided to aid your understanding.

1. LOGIC

SETS

This brief introduction to sets provides a basis for the study of logic. Later set theory is studied more formally. Apart from notation this section could be skipped by those previously exposed to the basic concepts of sets.

Symbolism. Braces are often used to name sets. For example, the set of integers 1, 2, 3, 4 could be named

$$\{1, 2, 3, 4\}.$$

This is the "roster" method for naming sets.

EXERCISES

1. Use the roster method to name the set which contains the numbers $\frac{5}{2}$, 2, and -1. ____________
2. The set $\{7, \pi, \sqrt{2}\}$ contains the numbers ______________.

ANSWERS:

1. $\{\frac{5}{2}, 2, -1\}$ 2. 7, π, $\sqrt{2}$

....

A method know as "set builder notation" is often used to name sets. A property is specified which is held by all objects in a set but not by any others. "P(x)", read "P of x", will denote a sentence referring to the variable x. For example,

$x = 23$
x is an even integer
$1 \le x \le 4$

The set of all objects x such that x satisfies P(x) is named

$$\{x \mid P(x)\}.$$

Then the set $\{1, 2, 3, 4\}$ can also be named

$$\{x \mid 1 \le x \le 4\}$$

which means

"The set of all x such that $1 \le x \le 4$."

EXERCISES

Use the roster method to name each set.

1. $\{x \mid x \text{ is an integer and } 1 \le x \le 8\}$ ____________
2. $\{y \mid y \text{ is an integer and } -4 \le y \le -1\}$ ____________
3. $\{x \mid x \text{ is an even integer}\}$ ____________
4. $\{x \mid x = 2k \text{ for some integer } k\}$ ____________

Use set builder notation to name each set.

5. $\{-1, 0, 1, 2\}$ ____________
6. $\{10, 11, 12, 13, \ldots\}$ ____________
7. $\{10, 20, 30, 40, \ldots\}$ ____________
8. $\{\frac{3}{2}\}$ ____________

ANSWERS:

1. $\{1, 2, 3, 4, 5, 6, 7, 8\}$ 2. $\{-4, -3, -2, -1\}$
3. $\{\ldots, -6, -4, -2, 0, 2, 4, 6, \ldots\}$
4. Same as 3
5. $\{x \mid -1 \le x \le 2\}$
6. $\{x \mid x > 9\}$ or $\{x \mid x \ge 10\}$
7. $\{x \mid x = 10 \cdot k \text{ for some natural number } k\}$

   or

   $\{x \mid x \text{ is a multiple of } 10\}$
8. $\{x \mid x = \frac{3}{2}\}$

. . . .

Henceforth, the words "object", "element", and "member" mean the same thing when referring to sets. For example, objects of sets are elements of sets and vice versa.

Membership. Sets will be denoted by capital letters and elements of sets by small letters. The expression

$$a \in A$$

means

a is an element of set A.

The following have the same meaning:

$a \in A$
a is in the set A
a is a member of the set A
a is an element of the set A

Similarly, "$x \notin A$" means "x is not an element of set A".

EXAMPLES. $1 \in \{1, 2, 3\}$
$5 \notin \{1, 2, 3\}$
$40 \in \{x \mid x \text{ is a multiple of } 10\}$.

EXERCISES

Place either '$\in$' or '$\notin$' in each blank to make a true sentence.

1. 1 ____ $\{2, 3\}$
2. 3 ____ $\{5, 7, 3, 2\}$
3. 2 ____ $\{x \mid x \text{ is an even integer}\}$
4. 15 ____ $\{x \mid x \text{ is an even integer}\}$

ANSWERS:

1. $\notin$ 2. $\in$ 3. $\in$ 4. $\notin$

....

<u>Subsets.</u> A is a subset of B if every element of A is also an element of B. The following have the same meaning:

$A \subset B$
Every element of A is an element of B.
Every member of A is a member of B.
A is included in B
B contains A
A is a subset of B

EXAMPLES. $\{1, 2, 3\} \subset \{1, 2, 3, 4\}$
$\{1, 3\} \subset \{1, 3\}$

A set is always a subset of itself; that is, for any set A, $A \subset A$. We prove this later. Also, $A \subset B$ means $B \supset A$.

EXERCISES

Place '$\subset$' or '$\supset$' in each blank to make a true sentence.

1. $\{8, 9\}$ ____ $\{7, 11, 9, 8\}$
2. $\{5, 4, 3, 2, 1\}$ ____ $\{1, 2, 3\}$

ANSWERS:

1. $\subset$ 2. $\supset$

....

<u>Equality for Sets.</u> If A and B represent sets, then A = B means that 'A' and 'B' represent the same set. The following have the same meaning:

A = B
A and B name the same set
A and B have precisely the same members
$A \subset B$ and $B \subset A$

EXAMPLES. $\{1, 2\} = \{x \mid (x-1)(x-2) = 0\}$
$\{1/2\} = \{x \mid 2x - 1 = 0\}$
$\{1, 2, 3\} = \{3, 2, 1\} = \{1, 2, 3, 3\}$

Note the order of listing elements is disregarded as well as repeated use of the same element.

EXERCISES

Pick out the pairs of sets which are equal.

$A = \{ x \mid x^2 = 3, x \text{ even} \}$
$B = \{ x \mid x^2 = 4 \}$
$C = \{ 7, 2, 4 \}$
$D = \{ 1, 2 \}$
$E = \{ 8, 9, 7, 4 \}$
$F = \{ 9, 9, 4, 7, 8 \}$
$G = \{ 2, 1 \}$
$H = \{ -2, 2 \}$

ANSWERS: $B = H$, $E = F$, $D = G$

....

The Empty Set. The set which contains no elements is known as the empty set and could be named '{ }', but we name it 'Ø'. For any set A, $\emptyset \subset A$. We prove this later.

EXERCISES

Which are true?

1. $\{x \mid x^2 = 3 \text{ and } x \text{ even}\} = \emptyset$
2. $\{1, 2\} = \emptyset$
3. $\{0\} = \emptyset$
4. $\{0\} \subset \emptyset$
5. $\emptyset \subset \{0\}$
6. $\emptyset \subset \{1, 2\}$

ANSWERS: 1, 5, and 6.

....

Intersections. The intersection of two sets A and B is the set of elements common to both sets. The intersection is symbolized

$$A \cap B$$

or

$$\{ x \mid x \in A \text{ and } x \in B \}.$$

EXAMPLES.
$\{1, 3\} \cap \{1, 2, 3, 4\} = \{1, 3\}$
$\{1, 3, 5\} \cap \{1, 2, 3, \ldots\} = \{1, 3, 5\}$
$\{x \mid x > 1\} \cap \{x \mid x > 2\} = \{x \mid x > 2\}$
$\{2, 4, 6, 8, \ldots\} \cap \{1, 3, 5, 7, \ldots\} = \emptyset$

In the last example there were no elements in common so the intersection is the empty set.

EXERCISES

Find each of the following intersections.

1. $\{1/2, 1\} \cap \{-4, 8\}$ ________
2. $\{3, 4, 5, 6, 7, \ldots\} \cap \{0, 1, 2, 3, 4\}$ ________
3. $\{1, 2, 3\} \cap \emptyset$ ________
4. $A \cap \emptyset$, for any set A ________
5. $\{x \mid x < 0\} \cap \{x \mid x < -1\}$ ________

ANSWERS:

1. $\emptyset$ 2. $\{3, 4\}$ 3. $\emptyset$ 4. $\emptyset$ 5. $\{x \mid x < -1\}$

....

Unions. The union of two sets A and B is the set of elements which are in A or B or both. The union is symbolized

$$A \cup B$$

or

$$\{x \mid x \in A \text{ or } x \in B \text{ or } x \in A \cap B\}.$$

EXAMPLES. $\{1, 2\} \cup \{3, 4, 5\} = \{1, 2, 3, 4, 5\}$
$\{2, 4, 6, 8, \ldots\} \cup \{1, 3, 5, 7, \ldots\} = \{1, 2, 3, \ldots\}$
$\{x \mid x > 1\} \cup \{x \mid x > 2\} = \{x \mid x > 1\}$

EXERCISES

Find each of the following unions.

1. $\{1/2, 1\} \cup \{-4, 8\}$ ________
2. $\{3, 4, 5, 6, 7, \ldots\} \cup \{0, 1, 2, 3, 4\}$ ________
3. $\{1, 2, 3\} \cup \emptyset$ ________
4. $A \cup \emptyset$, for any set A ________
5. $\{x \mid x < 0\} \cup \{x \mid x < -1\}$ ________

ANSWERS:

1. $\{1/2, 1, -4, 8\}$
2. $\{0, 1, 2, 3, 4, 5, \ldots\}$
3. $\{1, 2, 3\}$
4. A
5. $\{x \mid x < 0\}$

....

Universal Sets. Mathematicans always have a frame of reference called a universal set. In plane geometry the universal set is the set of all points in the plane. In solid geometry, the plane can no longer be used as the universal set. In calculus, we consider the set of real numbers, the set of real functions, the set of differentiable functions, and the set of continuous functions as universal sets. Usually it is clear what the universal set is, though you may have to decide what it is from the title of the book or the chapter you are studying, or from the context of the writing.

Complement. The *complement* of a set A is defined to be the set of all elements of the universal set which are not in A, and is symbolized

$$\complement A$$

EXAMPLE. If a universal set

$$U = \{2, 5, 7, 9, 11, 82\}$$

and

$$A = \{2, 9, 11, 82\}$$

then

$$\complement A = \{5, 7\}.$$

EXERCISES

If a universal set $U = \{1, 0, -1, 3, 5\}$, $A = \{-1, 0\}$, and $B = \{0, 3, 5\}$, find;

1. $\complement A$ ________	2. $A \cup \complement A$ ________
3. $A \cap \complement A$ ________	4. $\complement B$ ________
5. $B \cup \complement B$ ________	6. $B \cap \complement B$ ________

ANSWERS:

1. $\{1, 3, 5\}$ 2. U 3. $\emptyset$ 4. $\{1, -1\}$ 5. U 6. $\emptyset$

Note that $A \cup \complement A$ is always equal to the universal set and $A \cap \complement A$ is always equal to $\emptyset$. We prove this later.

Subsets of the Real Numbers. We will use the following capital letters to name specific subsets of the real numbers and refer to them as such throughout the book.

$N = \{1, 2, 3, 4, \ldots\}$ = The set of *natural* numbers
= The set of *positive integers*
= The counting numbers

$N_o = \{0\} \cup N = \{0, 1, 2, 3, 4, \ldots\}$ = The set of *nonnegative integers*
= The set of *whole numbers*

$I = \{\ldots, -3, -2, -1, 0, 1, 2, 3, \ldots\}$ = The set of *integers*

Notice that $N \subset N_o \subset I$.

$^{-}N = \{\ldots, -3, -2, -1\}$ = The set of *negative integers*

$P = \{p \mid p > 1$, p is a natural number, p is only divisible by 1 and p itself (has no proper divisors)$\}$

= The set of prime numbers

EXERCISES

List some elements of P ____________ .

ANSWERS: 2, 3, 5, 7, 11, 13, 17, 19

....

$Q = \{ a/b \mid a \in I \text{ and } b \in I \text{ and } b \neq 0 \}$ = The set of rational numbers.

EXAMPLES. $2/3 \in Q$, $-5/4 \in Q$

Notice $N \subset N_o \subset I \subset Q$, since $a/1 = a$ for any integer a.

$J = \{ x \mid x$ cannot be expressed as a ratio of two integers$\}$
= The set of irrational numbers.

EXAMPLES. $\sqrt{2} \in J$
$\pi \in J$
$e \in J$ $(e = 2.718\ldots)$
$2 \notin J$
$3/4 \notin J$

In fact $Q \cap J = \emptyset$

R = The set of real numbers
$= Q \cup J$

EXERCISES

1. If a universal set $U = \{ 0, 1, 2, 3, 10, 8 \}$,

$A = \{ 1, 2, 3, 10 \}$,
$B = \{ 0, 1, 8, 10 \}$,

and

$C = \{ 0, 1, 2, 3 \}$,

find the following.

a) $A \cap (B \cup C)$
b) $\complement A$
c) $\complement (A \cap B)$
d) $\complement (A \cap B \cap C)$
e) $\complement (A \cap (B \cup C))$
f) $\complement A \cup \complement B$
g) $(A \cap B) \cap C$
h) $A \cap (B \cap C)$
i) $(A \cup B) \cup C$
j) $A \cup (B \cup C)$

If R is the universal set find:

2. $Q \cap R$ ________
3. $I \cap J$ ________
4. $N \cap J$ ________
5. $N_o \cap J$ ________
6. $I \cap N$ ________
7. $\complement Q$ ________
8. $N_o \cup \bar{N}$ ________
9. $\complement J$ ________
10. Name $\{ x \mid x$ is an odd integer$\}$ in two other ways.

11. Suppose $D = \{ x \mid x \text{ is an odd integer} \}$ and
$E = \{ x \mid x \text{ is an even integer} \}$.

a) $D \cap E =$ ________ b) $D \cup E =$ ________

12. Name the following sets by the roster method.

a) $I_0 = \{ x \mid x \in I \text{ and } x = 3k \text{ for some } k \in I \}$

b) $I_1 = \{ x \mid x \in I \text{ and } x = 3k + 1 \text{ for some } k \in I \}$

c) $I_2 = \{ x \mid x \in I \text{ and } x = 3k + 2 \text{ for some } k \in I \}$

Then

d) $I_1 \cap I_0 =$ ________ e) $I_1 \cap I_2 =$ ________

f) $I_0 \cap I_2 =$ ________ g) $I_0 \cup I_1 \cup I_2 =$ ________

13. $\{ x \mid x^2 + 2x + 1 = 0 \} \cup \{ x \mid x^2 + 4x + 4 = 0 \} =$ ________

14. $\{ x \mid x \in R \text{ and } x^2 = -1 \} =$ ________

15. $\{ x \mid x \in J \text{ and } x \in Q \} =$ ________

Use the roster method to describe the sets in Exercises 16 through 18.

16. $\{ x \mid x \text{ is an integer and } x \text{ is not even} \} =$ ________

17. $\{ x \mid x \text{ is an integer and } x \text{ is not odd} \} =$ ________

18. $\{ x \mid x \text{ is an even integer and } x \text{ is prime} \} =$ ________

19. The intervals are important subsets of R. They are defined and described on the real line as follows:

$[a, b] = \{ x \mid a \le x \le b \}$

$[a, b) = \{ x \mid a \le x < b \}$

$(a, b] = \{ x \mid a < x \le b \}$

$(a, b) = \{ x \mid a < x < b \}$

$(a, \infty) = \{ x \mid a < x \}$

$[a, \infty) = \{ x \mid a \le x \}$

$(-\infty, a) = \complement [a, \infty)$

$(-\infty, a] = \complement (a, \infty)$

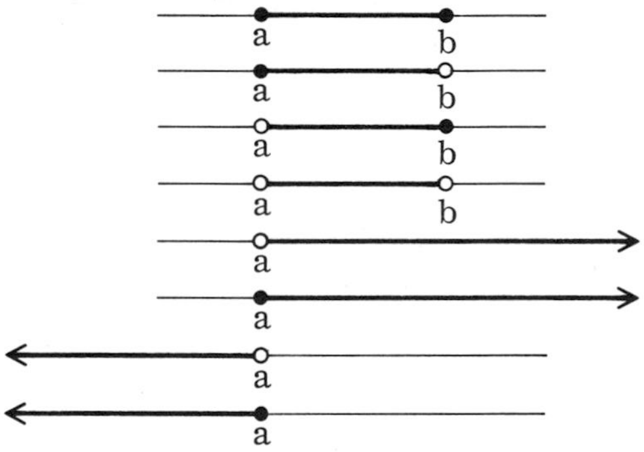

Find:

a) $(-\infty, 3) \cap [2, \infty)$ ________

b) $(-\infty, 3) \cup [3, \infty)$ ________

c) $[-1, 2) \cup [1, 4)$ ________

d) $[-1, 2) \cap [1, 4)$ ________

e) $[3, 3]$ ________

f) $(3, 3)$ ________

g) $[-n, n] \cap [-(n+1), n+1]$ ________

h) $[-n, n] \cup [-(n+1), n+1]$ ________

20. If U is a set, then $\mathcal{P}(U)$, the <u>power set</u> of U, is $\{ A \mid A \subset U \}$. For example, $\mathcal{P}(\{a, b\}) = \{ \emptyset, \{a\}, \{b\}, \{a, b\} \}$. Note that $\mathcal{P}(U)$ is a set whose elements are sets. Find:

a) $\mathcal{P}(\{1, 2\})$
b) $\mathcal{P}(\{0\})$
c) $\mathcal{P}(\{1, 2, 3\})$
d) $\mathcal{P}(\emptyset)$

ANSWERS:

1. a) A b) $\{0, 8\}$
   c) $\{0, 2, 3, 8\}$ d) $\{0, 2, 3, 10, 8\}$
   e) $\{0, 8\}$ f) $\{0, 8, 2, 3\}$
   g) $\{1\}$ h) $\{1\}$
   i) U j) U
2. Q 3. $\emptyset$ 4. $\emptyset$ 5. $\emptyset$ 6. N 7. J
8. I 9. Q
10. $\{x \mid x = 2k+1, \text{ for some integer } k\}$, or
    $\{\ldots, -5, -3, -1, 1, 3, 5, 7, \ldots\}$
11. a) $\emptyset$ b) I
12. a) $\{\ldots, -9, -6, -3, 0, 3, 6, 9, \ldots\}$
    b) $\{\ldots, -7, -4, -1, 1, 4, 7, 10, \ldots\}$
    c) $\{\ldots, -8, -5, -2, 2, 5, 8, 11, \ldots\}$
    d) $\emptyset$ e) $\emptyset$ f) $\emptyset$ g) I
13. $\{-1, -2\}$ 14. $\emptyset$ 15. $\emptyset$
16. $\{\ldots, -1, 1, 3, \ldots\}$
17. $\{\ldots, -2, 0, 2, \ldots\}$
18. $\{2\}$
19. a) $[2, 3)$ b) R
    c) $[-1, 4)$ d) $[1, 2)$
    e) $\{3\}$ f) $\emptyset$
    g) $[-n, n]$ h) $[-(n+1), n+1]$
20. b) $\{\emptyset, \{0\}\}$ d) $\{\emptyset\}$

....

SENTENCES

Logic and mathematical proofs can be studied just like algebra, geometry, or calculus. To study logic is to study the language of mathematics.

Just as everyone uses sentences to convey ideas, mathematicians use sentences to convey their ideas; for example,

$$x + y = 1,$$
$$2 + 3 = 5,$$
$$\int_0^3 \cos x \, dx = \sin 3,$$

and so on.

Statements. Declarative sentences which are true or false, but not both, are called statements. The following are statements.

Roger Maris hit 61 home runs in one season.	(true)
$2 + 3 = 6$	(false)

$7 - 2 = 5$ (true)

For every x, if, $f(x) = \sin x$, then $f'(x) = \cos x$ (true)

The following are not statements.

Why are you studying mathematics?
He is a baseball player.
$x + 1 = 0$
$k - m = b$

Variables. The sentence

He is a baseball player,

cannot be judged true or false because we do not know who He is. If the word 'He' is replaced by 'Richard Nixon' forming the sentence

Richard Nixon is a baseball player

the sentence becomes a (false) statement. Similarly, if 'x' in the sentence

$x + 1 = 0$

is replaced by '3', forming the sentence

$\underline{3} + 1 = 0,$

the sentence then becomes a (false) statement.

The letter 'x' is a variable in the sentence $x + 1 = 0$. A letter (or other symbol) that can represent various elements of a universal set is called a variable. Thus, 'He' is a variable in the sentence

He is a baseball player.

EXERCISES

Consider the following sentences for the exercises.

a) $x < 2$

b) $\lim_{n \to \infty} n = 1$

c) $x + y = y + x$

d) There exists a natural number x such that $x < 2$.

e) For every real number x and every real number y, $x + y = y + x$.

f) $1 < 2$

g) $2 + 3 = 3 + 2$

h) This sentence is false.

1. Which of the above are statements?
2. Identify the variables in each sentence.
3. Which will become statements when the variables are replaced by numbers?

ANSWERS:

1. b, d, e, f, and g
2. a) x b) n c) x, y d) x e) x, y 3. a, c

From the preceding exercises it follows that we can make a sentence a statement by replacing its variables by numbers or by attaching phrases such as "For every" or "There exists" to the sentence. For example,

$x < 3$

is not a statement, but each of the following is a statement:

$1 < 3$
$5 < 3$
For every real number x, $x < 3$
There exists an x such that $x < 3$

Solution Sets. Replacements for variables of a sentence are always chosen from some universal set.

EXAMPLE. Replace the variable in the sentence

$x + 1 < 3$

by each element of the universal set $\{0, 1, 2, 3\}$ and decide the truth value of resulting sentence.

$0 + 1 < 3$	(true)
$1 + 1 < 3$	(true)
$2 + 1 < 3$	(false)
$3 + 1 < 3$	(false)

Any replacement which makes a sentence true is called a solution. The set of all solutions is called the solution set of the sentence. In the above example the solution set is $\{0, 1\}$.

You probably know other more direct ways of finding solution sets using algebra.

EXERCISES

Find the solution set of each sentence with indicated universal set.

1. $x - 2 < 3$	$\{0, 1, 2, 3\}$
2. $\|x\| + 1 < 3$	$\{0, 1, 2, 3\}$
3. $(x-1)(x+2) = 0$	$\{5, 6, 7\}$
4. $(x-1)(x+2) = 0$	$\{-2, -1, 0, 1, 2\}$
5. $x^2 + 2x + 1 = 0$	N
6. $x^2 + 2x + 1 = 0$	I
7. $2x^2 + 3x + 1 = 0$	N
8. $2x^2 + 3x + 1 = 0$	$\bar{N}$
9. $2x^2 + 3x + 1 = 0$	I
10. $2x^2 + 3x + 1 = 0$	Q
11. $2x^2 + 3x + 1 = 0$	R
12. $x^2 + 1 = 0$	R

13. $\frac{x^2 - 4}{x + 2} = (x - 2)$ R

ANSWERS:

1. $\{0, 1, 2, 3\}$
2. $\{0, 1\}$
3. $\emptyset$
4. $\{1, -2\}$
5. $\emptyset$
6. $\{-1\}$
7. $\emptyset$
8. $\{-1\}$
9. $\{-1\}$
10. $\{-1, -\frac{1}{2}\}$
11. $\{-1, -\frac{1}{2}\}$
12. $\emptyset$
13. $\{x \mid x \in R \text{ and } x \neq -2\}$

....

From now on we consider only sentences which are statements or statement forms which become statements when meaningful replacements are made for all of their variables.

When doing proofs we may consider a sentence like

If $x = 11$, then $3x = 33$

to be a statement because we have assumed x represents an element of a universal set.

EXERCISES

Decide the truth value of each of the following. Refer to a calculus book where appropriate. Assume that x represents a real number, and f represents a real function.

1. For every real number x, $x^2 = 0$.
2. If $x = 3$, then $x < 2$.
3. If $f(x) = x^2$, then $f'(x) = 2x$.
4. If $x = 0$ or $x = 1$, then $x^2 = x$.
5. For every natural number x, $x^2 = x$.
6. There exists a natural number x such that $x^2 = x$.
7. $\sqrt{x^2} = |x|$.
8. If $|x| < 3$, then $-3 < x < 3$.
9. Every rational number can be expressed as a ratio of two integers.
10. If $f(x) = |x|$, then f is continuous but not differentiable.
11. The series $\sum_{n=1}^{\infty} (-1)^n n^{-1}$ is convergent but not absolutely convergent.
12. If a series is absolutely convergent, then it is convergent.

13. A series either converges or diverges.
14. If a function is continuous, then it is differentiable.
15. $\lim_{n \to \infty} n^{-1} = 1$
16. For every real number x and every real number y, $x + y = 0$
17. If a function is differentiable, then it is continuous.
18. There exists a real number x such that $x < 2$.

ANSWERS:

1. False, $1^2 \neq 0$	2. False
3. True	4. True
5. False, $2^2 \neq 2$	6. True
7. True	8. True
9. True	10. True
11. True	12. True
13. True	14. False, See Exercise 10.
15. False	16. False, $2 + 3 \neq 0$
17. True	18. True, $x = 0$ or 1

....

SENTENCE CONNECTIVES

Conjunction. If P and Q are sentences, then the sentence 'P and Q' is called the conjunction of P and Q, symbolized

$$P \wedge Q.$$

For any sentence there are just two possible truth values, true (T) or false (F). If P and Q are both true, then $P \wedge Q$ is true. If one or both of P and Q are false, then $P \wedge Q$ is false. The truth table below defines the truth values of $P \wedge Q$ for all possible truth value combinations of P and Q.

P	Q	$P \wedge Q$
T	T	T
F	T	F
T	F	F
F	F	F

EXAMPLE. $2 + 2 = 4 \wedge 3 + 2 = 7$ (false)
π is irrational $\wedge\ \pi < 0$ (true)

EXERCISES

Find the truth value.

1. $\lim_{n \to \infty} (1/n) = 1 \wedge$ e is rational __________
2. For every x, $\sqrt{x^2} = |x| \wedge 4 \neq 3$ __________

ANSWERS:

1. F   2. T

....

<u>Disjunction</u>. If P and Q are sentences, then the sentence 'P or Q' is called the <u>disjunction</u> of P and Q, symbolized

$$P \vee Q.$$

Unlike conjunctions there are at least two uses of "or" in English.

One use is exclusive, meaning "one or the other but not both". For example, the sentence

Are you awake or asleep?

cannot be answered <u>yes</u> because you cannot be both awake and asleep at the same time.

Another use is inclusive, meaning "and/or". For example, the sentence

Are you wearing a shirt or sweater?

could be answered <u>yes</u>. This would mean the answerer was wearing either a shirt, a sweater, or both.

The mathematician <u>defines</u> "or" to be inclusive; that is $P \vee Q$ is true when P is true, Q is true, or both are true. $P \vee Q$ is false just when P and Q are false. The truth table for $P \vee Q$ is thus defined below.

P	Q	$P \vee Q$
T	T	T
T	F	T
F	T	T
F	F	F

EXAMPLE. "$2 + 2 = 4 \vee 3 + 2 = 5$" is true because both are true.
"π is rational $\vee$ π is irrational" is true because "π is irrational" is true.

EXERCISES

Find the truth value.

1. π is rational $\vee$ π is real. ________
2. π is an integer $\vee$ π is a natural number. ________
3. $J \cap Q = R \vee \int \sin x \, dx = \cos x + c$. ________
4. $S = \sum_{n=1}^{\infty} u_n$ is an infinite series; S converges $\vee$ S diverges. ________

ANSWERS:

1. T   2. F   3. F   4. T

....

<u>Negation.</u> A negative, or denial, of a sentence is formed in many ways. For example, if P is

Chicago is a city,

the negation of P is represented by each of the following.

$\sim P$
Chicago is <u>not</u> a city
It is false that Chicago is a city
It is not true that Chicago is a city

As another example, the negation of

P: 2 is rational,

is represented by each of the following.

$\sim P$
It is false that 2 is rational
2 is not rational
2 is irrational

The truth table for negation is defined below.

P	$\sim P$
T	F
F	T

<u>Definition.</u> $a \neq b$ means $\sim (a = b)$
$\sim (a < b)$ means $a \geq b$
$a \notin A$ means $\sim (a \in A)$

EXERCISES

Write four different representations of the negations of each.

1. P: $2 = 3$
2. P: e is irrational

Find the truth value of each.

3. $2 \neq 3$
4. $\sim$ (e is irrational)

Give an expression for each of the following which does not involve a negation symbol.

5. $\sim (x < y)$
6. $\sim (x > y)$
7. $\sim (3 \leq y)$
8. $\sim (z^2 \geq 1 + x)$

ANSWERS:

1. $\sim P$

$\sim (2 = 3)$

$2 \neq 3$

It is false that $2 = 3$

It is not true that $2 = 3$

2. $\sim P$

e is not irrational

e is rational

It is false that e is irrational

It is not true that e is irrational

3. T

4. F

5. $x \geq y$

6. $x \leq y$

7. $3 > y$

8. $z^2 < 1 + x$

••

Conditional. If P and Q are sentences, the sentence

If P, then Q

is symbolized

$P \rightarrow Q$.

The mathematician defines a truth table for $P \rightarrow Q$ just as he does for $\sim$, $\wedge$, and $\vee$. But, the definition is not at all obvious. An example may help first. Consider the sentence

If I get an A in mathematics, then I will take the next course.

Suppose a fellow student says this. When is he telling the truth and when is he lying? Examine the following four cases where

P means "I get an A in mathematics"

and

Q means "I will take the next course".

1) P (true): He gets an A in mathematics
   Q (true): He takes the next course
2) P (true): He gets an A in mathematics
   Q (false): He does not take the next course
3) P (false): He does not get the A
   Q (true): He takes the next course
4) P (false): He does not get the A
   Q (false): He does not take the course

In (1) it is reasonable to agree that the student was telling the truth; his claim is true. In (2) it is easy to agree that he lied, and his claim was false. In (3) you could not call him a liar since he takes the next course even though he did not get an A. In (4) you likewise could not call him a liar since he did not get the A and did not take the next course.

The truth table definition for $P \rightarrow Q$ conforms to the previous example. There is nothing to debate about the definition, it is an agreement among mathematicians.

	P	Q	P → Q
1)	T	T	T
2)	T	F	F
3)	F	T	T
4)	F	F	T

The numbers refer to the example.

The sentence $P \rightarrow Q$ is called a conditional with

P the antecedent

and

Q the consequent.

To summarize, a conditional is true when the antecedent is false or the consequent is true. A conditional is false only when the antecedent is true and the consequent is false.

EXERCISES

Find the truth value.

1. $2 < 1 \rightarrow 2 < 3$ ____
2. $3 > 4 \rightarrow 6 < 5$ ____
3. $2 = \sqrt{4} \rightarrow \sum_{n=1}^{\infty} n^{-1}$ converges ____
4. $2 \geq 0 \rightarrow \sum_{n=1}^{\infty} n^{-2}$ converges ____

ANSWERS:

1. T   2. T   3. F   4. T

....

In mathematics $P \rightarrow Q$ is encountered in many forms. You should be familiar with each. The following have the same meaning:

P → Q
If P, then Q
P implies Q
Q if P, P only if Q
Q provided P
Q whenever P, Q when P
P is a sufficient condition for Q
Q is necessary condition for P

[Memorize these]

One meaning of

$P \rightarrow Q$

is

"P is sufficient for Q".

This can be explained via its truth table. When P is true and $P \rightarrow Q$ is true, then Q must be true. In other words P being true is enough (is sufficient) to yield Q being true when $P \rightarrow Q$ is true.

Another meaning of

$P \rightarrow Q$

is

"Q is a necessary condition for P".

This is also explained via the truth table for $P \rightarrow Q$. If $P \rightarrow Q$ is true and Q is false, then P must be false; that is, if Q is false, so is P. Q being false necessitates P being false.

EXAMPLES. Translate to the form $P \rightarrow Q$.

a) A polygon has no diagonals, only if it is a triangle.

Using the following translations:

P: A polygon has no diagonals
Q: It is a triangle

the sentence translates to a sentence of the type $P \rightarrow Q$, or

If a polygon has no diagonals, then it is a triangle.

b) The function f is continuous when it is differentiable.

Using the following translations:

P: A function is differentiable
Q: A function is continuous,

the sentence translates to the type $P \rightarrow Q$, or

If a function is differentiable, then it is continuous

Experience at recognizing sentences with "If, then" structure, though not stated as such, will aid mathematical reading and proof.

EXERCISES

Translate each sentence to the type "If P, then Q" and $P \rightarrow Q$. Identify the antecedent and the consequent.

1. There is no factorization of n whenever n is prime.

2. $\sum_{n=1}^{\infty} u_n$ converges only if $\lim_{n \rightarrow \infty} u_n = 0$.

3. $|r| < 1$ implies that $\lim_{n \to \infty} (a + ar + \ldots + ar^n) = a/(1 - r)$
4. x is an integer if it is a natural number. [Use set symbols I, N]
5. If $\sum_{n=1}^{\infty} |u_n|$ converges, so does $\sum_{n=1}^{\infty} u_n$.
6. The convergence of $\sum_{n=1}^{\infty} |u_n|$ is sufficient for the convergence of $\sum_{n=1}^{\infty} u_n$.
7. $a \in R$ is a necessary condition for $a \in Q$.
8. An integer is a rational number. Hint: Use a variable x and set symbols; e.g., I, Q.
9. Integers are rationals.
10. A necessary condition for lines ℓ_1 and ℓ_2 to be parallel is that $\ell_1 \cap \ell_2 = \emptyset$.
11. A square is a rectangle.
12. Triangles are polygons.
13. $3x = 3y$ since $x = y$.
14. $f'(x) = 2x$ when $f(x) = x^2$.
15. Squares are not triangles.

ANSWERS:

In the following $P \to Q$ can replace "If P, then Q"; and vice versa.

1. If n is prime, then n has no factorization.
2. If $\sum_{n=1}^{\infty} u_n$ converges, then $\lim_{n \to \infty} u_n = 0$.
3. If $|r| < 1$, then $\lim_{n \to \infty} (a + ar + \ldots + ar^n) = a/(1 - r)$.
4. If $x \in N$, then $x \in I$.
5. If $\sum_{n=1}^{\infty} |u_n|$ converges, then $\sum_{n=1}^{\infty} u_n$ converges.
6. Same as 5.
7. $a \in Q \to a \in R$.
8. $x \in I \to x \in Q$.
9. Same as 8.
10. ℓ_1 parallel to $\ell_2 \to \ell_1 \cap \ell_2 = \emptyset$
11. x is a square $\to$ x is a rectangle.
12. x is a triangle $\to$ x is a polygon.

13. $x = y \to 3x = 3y$.

14. $f(x) = x^2 \to f'(x) = 2x$.

15. x is a square → x is not a triangle.

. . . .

Biconditional. A sentence of the type

$$(P \to Q) \wedge (Q \to P)$$

is called a biconditional, symbolized

$$P \leftrightarrow Q.$$

When P and Q are sentences the truth table for $P \leftrightarrow Q$ is

P	Q	$P \leftrightarrow Q$
T	T	T
T	F	F
F	T	F
F	F	T

and is derived from the truth tables for → and ∧.

EXERCISES

1. Complete the following truth table.

P	Q	$P \to Q$	$Q \to P$
T	T	____	____
T	F	____	____
F	T	____	____
F	F	____	____

2. The truth table for $P \leftrightarrow Q$ then follows; complete it.

$P \to Q$	$Q \to P$	$(P \to Q) \wedge (Q \to P)$ or $P \leftrightarrow Q$
T	T	____
F	T	____
T	F	____
T	T	____

ANSWERS:

2. T; F; F; T.

. . . .

Thus, $P \leftrightarrow Q$ is true when P and Q are both true or both false.

EXERCISES

Find the truth value.

1. $2 < 1 \leftrightarrow 2 < 3$ ____

2. π is real $\leftrightarrow$ π is irrational. ____
3. 2 is real $\leftrightarrow$ 2 is irrational. ____
4. 2 is real $\leftrightarrow$ 2 is rational. ____
5. e is rational $\leftrightarrow$ e is an integer. ___

ANSWERS:

1. F 2. T 3. F 4. T 5. F

....

In mathematics $P \leftrightarrow Q$ is encountered in many forms. The following have the same meaning:

$P \leftrightarrow Q$
P is equivalent to Q
P is necessary and sufficient condition for Q
Q is necessary and sufficient condition for P
P if and only if Q
Q if and only if P
P iff Q ("iff" is an abbreviation for "if and only if")
If P, then Q and conversely
If Q, then P and conversely

[Memorize these]

For example,

$5x = 15$ if and only if $x = 3$

would be translated by

P: $5x = 15$
Q: $x = 3$

to

$P \leftrightarrow Q.$

A meaning of

$P \leftrightarrow Q$

is

"P is a necessary and sufficient condition for Q".

This is explained via the definition of

$P \leftrightarrow Q$: $(P \rightarrow Q) \wedge (Q \rightarrow P)$.

If P is a necessary condition for Q, then $Q \rightarrow P$. If P is a sufficient condition for Q, then $P \rightarrow Q$.

EXERCISES

Translate to a sentence of the type $P \leftrightarrow Q$.

1. $x = 5$ if and only if $2x = 10$.
2. $x \in Q$ is a necessary and sufficient condition for $x = p/q$ where $p \in I$, $q \in I$, and $q \neq 0$.
3. A necessary and sufficient condition for the sequence $\{x_n\}_{n=1}^{\infty}$ to have a limit is that the absolute value $|x_n - x_m|$ approach 0 as m and n go to infinity.
4. $ab = 0$ if and only if $a = 0$ or $b = 0$.
5. If a triangle is isosceles, then it must have two sides equal and conversely.
6. $2x - 1 = 0$ is equivalent to $x = \frac{1}{2}$.
7. f is continuous if and only if f is differentiable.

ANSWERS:

1. $x = 5 \leftrightarrow 2x = 10$.
2. $x \in Q \leftrightarrow (x = p/q$ where $p \in I \wedge q \in I \wedge q \neq 0)$
3. $\{x_n\}_{n=1}^{\infty}$ has a limit $\leftrightarrow$ $|x_m - x_n| \rightarrow 0$ as m, n got to infinity.
4. $ab = 0 \leftrightarrow (a = 0 \vee b = 0)$.
5. A triangle is isosceles $\leftrightarrow$ two sides are equal.
   If we used a variable x for triangle we could translate the sentence as:
   x is isosceles $\leftrightarrow$ x has two sides equal.
6. $2x - 1 = 0 \leftrightarrow x = 1/2$.
7. f is continuous $\leftrightarrow$ f is differentiable.

....

<u>Combination of Connectives.</u> Combinations of , $\rightarrow$, $\leftrightarrow$, $\wedge$ and $\vee$ often occur. A facility at recognizing them is essential for mathematical reading and proof.

EXAMPLE. We could translate

If p is prime, then if p is even p must be smaller than 7

as follows:

P: p is prime
Q: p is even
R: p must be smaller than 7.

The translated sentence would be

$$P \rightarrow (Q \rightarrow R);$$

that is,

P implies that Q implies R.

EXAMPLE. Translate

"If a is perpendicular to c and b is perpendicular to c, then a is parallel to c".

Let

P: a is perpendicular to c,
Q: b is perpendicular to c,

and

R: a is parallel to c,

then the translated sentence is

$(P \wedge Q) \rightarrow R$.

EXAMPLE. Translate

"If lines l and m are not parallel, then l and m intersect".

Let

P: lines l and m are parallel
Q: l and m intersect,

then the translated sentence is

$\sim P \rightarrow Q$

not P implies Q.

You could have let

R: lines l and m are <u>not</u> parallel,

then the translated sentence would have been

$R \rightarrow Q$.

The first translation is more desirable because it reveals more logical structure.

EXERCISES

Translate using $\rightarrow$, $\leftrightarrow$, $\sim$, $\wedge$, and $\vee$.

1. If p and q are integers and $q \neq 0$, then p/q is a rational number.
2. If ABC is a triangle and ABC is isosceles, then ABC has two equal sides.
3. If a, b, c, and x are real numbers, $a \neq 0$, $ax^2 + bx + c = 0$, and $b^2 - 4ac = 0$, then the roots of $ax^2 + bx + c = 0$ are real and equal.
4. If a series $\sum_{n=1}^{\infty} u_n$ is convergent, then $\lim_{n\rightarrow\infty} u_n = 0$.
5. If u_n does not approach 0 as $n \rightarrow \infty$, then the series $\sum_{n=1}^{\infty} u_n$ cannot be convergent.

6. If a is an integer, then a is even or a is odd.
7. f is differentiable and g is differentiable only if $g \circ f$ is differentiable.
8. If u and v are differentiable functions of x, uv is also differentiable and $d(uv)/dx = u(dv/dx) + v(du/dx)$.
9. $x \in J$ or $x \in Q$ is a necessary and sufficient condition for $x \in R$.
10. $x \in {}^{-}N$ or $x \in N_o$ is equivalent to $x \in I$.
11. $x \in A \cap B$ iff ($x \in A$ and $x \in B$)
12. $x \in A \cup B$ iff ($x \in A$ or $x \in B$)
13. $x \in \complement A$ is a necessary and sufficient condition for $x \notin A$.

ANSWERS:

1. $(p \in I \wedge q \in I \wedge q \neq 0) \rightarrow p/q \in Q$
2. (ABC is a triangle $\wedge$ ABC is a isosceles) $\rightarrow$ ABC has two equal sides.
3. (a, b, c, and x are real numbers $\wedge$ $a \neq 0 \wedge ax^2 + bx + c = 0 \wedge b^2 = 4ac = 0$) $\rightarrow$ the roots of $ax^2 + bx + c = 0$ are real and equal.
4. $\sum_{n=1}^{\infty} u_n$ is convergent $\rightarrow \lim_{n=1} u_n = 0$.
5. $\lim_{n \rightarrow \infty} u_n \neq 0 \rightarrow \sum_{n=1}^{\infty} u_n$ is not convergent.
6. $a \in I \rightarrow$ (a is even $\vee$ a is odd)
7. (f is differentiable $\wedge$ g is differentiable) $\rightarrow g \circ f$ is differentiable.
8. (u and v are differentiable functions of x) $\rightarrow$ [uv is also differentiable $\wedge\ d(uv)/dx = u\frac{dv}{dx} + v\frac{du}{dx}$]
9. $(x \in J \vee x \in Q) \leftrightarrow x \in R$
10. $(x \in {}^{-}N \vee x \in N_o) \leftrightarrow x \in I$
11. $x \in A \cap B \leftrightarrow (x \in A \wedge x \in B)$
12. $x \in A \cup B \leftrightarrow (x \in A \vee x \in B)$
13. $x \in \complement A \leftrightarrow x \notin A$.

QUANTIFIERS

Sentences involving the phrases "For every ..." and "There exists ..." also play an important role in the structure of mathematical sentences. For example, the sentences

For every x, $x + 0 = x$

and

There exists an x such that $x^2 = 2$

express certain properties of the real number system.

<u>The Universal Quantifier.</u> The symbol '$\forall$', called the <u>universal quantifier</u> symbolizes phrases such as "For each", "For all", and "For every". A sentence such as

For every x, P(x)

translates to

$\forall x$, P(x)

The following have the same meaning.

$\forall x$, x is an integer $\rightarrow$ x $\in$ Q
For every x, if x is an integer, then x $\in$ Q
For all x, if x is an integer, then x $\in$ Q
For each x, if x is an integer, then x $\in$ Q
Every integer belongs to Q

EXERCISES

Translate.

1. Every triangle is a polygon.
2. For every x, if x is a natural number, then x is an integer.
3. For each natural number x, x is even or x is odd.

ANSWERS:

1. $\forall x$, x is a triangle $\rightarrow$ x is a polygon.
2. $\forall x$, x is a natural number $\rightarrow$ x is an integer.
3. $\forall x$[x is a natural number $\rightarrow$ (x is even $\vee$ x is odd)]

....

In some mathematics books a sentence like

If x is an integer, then x $\in$ Q

is understood to mean

$\forall x$, x is an integer $\rightarrow$ x $\in$ Q

That is, the universal quantifier is understood and not written. This is pointed out to enable you to interpret sentences you read since each author has his own style of writing.

As another example, in trigonometry the sentences

$\sin^2 u + \cos^2 u \equiv 1$

and

$\sin^2 u + \cos^2 u = 1$

mean

$\forall u$, $\sin^2 u + \cos^2 u = 1$,

where the quantifier refers to the set of real numbers

EXERCISES

What might "$\sqrt{x^2} = |x|$" mean if you encountered it in a text?

ANSWER:

$\forall x, \sqrt{x^2} = |x|$

....

The sentence

For every x, x is real

could be translated by:

R(x): x is real

to

$\forall x$, R(x)

The symbol 'R(x)' is used in place of "x is real" to reveal the structure of the sentence.

Let

U(x): $x \in Q$
R(x): x is real

then

For every x, if x is real, then $x \in Q$.

translates to

$\forall x$, R(x) $\rightarrow$ U(x).

EXERCISES

Translate using $\rightarrow$, $\leftrightarrow$, $\sim$, $\wedge$, $\vee$, $\forall$, and variables.

1. Every triangle is a polygon.
2. For every x, if x is a natural number, then x is an integer.
3. For every natural number y, y is even or y is odd.
4. For each function f, if f is continuous and differentiable, then f can be integrated.
5. Every function is either continuous or discontinuous.

ANSWERS:

1. $\forall$x(x is a triangle $\rightarrow$ x is a polygon)
2. $\forall$x($x \in N \rightarrow x \in I$)
3. $\forall$y[$y \in N \rightarrow$ (y is even $\vee$ y is odd)]
4. $\forall f$ [(f is continuous $\wedge$ f is differentiable) $\rightarrow$ f can be integrated]

5. $\forall f$ (f is continuous $\vee$ f is discontinuous)

....

The Existential Quantifier. The symbol '$\exists$', called the existential quantifier symbolizes phrases such as "There exists", "There is at least one", "For at least one", and "Some". A sentence such as

There exists an x such that P(x)

translates to

$\exists$ x, P(x).

The following have the same meaning.

$\exists$ x(x is a natural number)
There exists an x such that x is a natural number
Some number is natural
There is at least one natural number

It is important to realize that '$\exists$' means "There exists at least one"; there is nothing to prevent there being more. For example, compare the sentences

$\exists$ x(x = 0)

and

$\exists$ f (f is continuous).

For

$\exists$ x(x = 0)

we know there is only one x such that x = 0, but for

$\exists$ f (f is continuous)

we know there is at least one, in fact many functions which are continuous.

EXERCISES

Translate.

1. There exists an x such that x is prime and x is even.
2. There is an x such that $x = \lim_{n\to\infty} (1/n)$.
3. There is an X such that $n \le X \le 2$ and $\int_n^2 f(x)dx = (2 - n) f(X)$.

ANSWERS:

1. $\exists$ x(x is prime $\wedge$ x is even)
2. $\exists$ x[$x = \lim_{n\to\infty} (1/n)$]

3. $\exists X[n \leq X \leq 2 \wedge \int_n^2 f(x)dx = (2-n)f(X)]$

....

Combinations of Quantifiers. Quantifiers may appear together. Consider the following examples. The sentences

For every x and for every y, x + y = 0

translates to

$\forall x \forall y,\ x + y = 0.$

The sentence

For every x there exists a y such that x + y = 0

translates to

$\forall x \exists y,\ x + y = 0.$

The sentence

There exists an x such that for every y, x + y = 0

translates to

$\exists x \forall y,\ x + y = 0.$

The sentence

There exists an x and there exists a y such that x + y = 0

translates to

$\exists x \exists y,\ x + y = 0.$

EXERCISES

Translate to logical symbolism.

1. There exists a p and there exists a q such that $p \cdot q = 32$.
2. For every x there exists a y such that $x < y$.
3. There exists a y such that for every x, $x + 0 = y$.
4. There exists a x and there exists a y such that x^y is irrational.
5. For every x and for every y, $x + y = y + x$.
6. There exists an x and y such that $x^2 = y$.
7. For every x and y, $xy = yx$.

ANSWERS:

1. $\exists p \exists q,\ p \cdot q = 32.$
2. $\forall x \exists y,\ x < y.$
3. $\exists y \forall x,\ x + 0 = y.$
4. $\exists x \exists y$, x^y is irrational.

5. $\forall x \forall y,\ x + y = y + x.$
6. $\exists x \exists y,\ x^2 = y.$
7. $\forall x \forall y,\ xy = yx.$

....

Quantifiers may not appear together. For example, the sentence

For every x, if x is even, then there exists a y such that $x = 2y$.

translates to

$\forall x(x \text{ is even} \rightarrow \exists y,\ x = 2y)$

EXERCISES

Translate.

1. For every n there exists an m such that $n < m$.
2. $1 < 2 \rightarrow$ there exists an x such that $x < 2$.
3. For every x, $\sqrt{x} = k$ implies that there is a y such that $\sqrt{y} = k$.

Translate using $\wedge$, $\vee$, $\sim$, $\rightarrow$, $\exists$, $\forall$, and the following symbols for sentences.

D(f): f is differentiable
C(f): f is continuous
T(x): x is a triangle
P(x): x is a polygon
S(x): x is a square
R(x): x is a rectangle
E(x): x is an equilateral triangle
A(x): x is an equiangular triangle
V(x): x is even
O(x): x is odd
I(f): f is integrable
L(x): x is isosceles

4. Every differentiable function is continuous.
5. There are continuous functions which are not differentiable.
6. All equilateral triangles are equiangular and some equiangular triangles are equilateral.
7. If every number which is even is not odd, then some odd numbers cannot be even.
8. If all equilateral triangles are isosoceles, then some isosceles triangles are not equilateral.
9. All squares are rectangles.
10. Some triangles are equilateral.
11. Some equilateral triangles are polygons but not all polygons are equilateral triangles.
12. Every function is continuous or discontinuous.
13. Every even number is not odd.

ANSWERS:

1. $\forall n \exists m(n < m)$
2. $1 < 2 \rightarrow \exists x(x < 2)$
3. $\forall x(\sqrt{x} = k) \rightarrow \exists y(\sqrt{y} = k)$
4. $\forall f, D(f) \rightarrow C(f)$
5. $\exists f, C(f) \wedge \sim D(f)$
6. $\forall x, E(x) \rightarrow A(x) \wedge \exists x, A(x) \rightarrow E(x)$
7. $\forall x, [V(x) \rightarrow \sim O(x)] \rightarrow [\exists x, O(x) \wedge \sim V(x)]$
8. $\forall x, E(x) \rightarrow L(x) \rightarrow \exists x, L(x) \wedge \sim E(x)$
9. $\forall x, S(x) \rightarrow R(x)$
10. $\exists x, E(x)$
11. $\exists x[E(x) \rightarrow P(x) \wedge \sim \forall x[P(x) \rightarrow E(x)]$
12. $\forall f, C(f) \vee \sim C(f)$
13. $\forall x, E(x) \rightarrow \sim O(x)$

....

Truth Values of Quantified Sentences. Quantifiers refer to a universal set. Sometimes the universal set is pointed out, but sometimes it must be inferred from context. For example, consider the sentence

$\forall x$, x is a traingle $\rightarrow$ x is a polygon

The universal set might be the set of figures in the plane, or could be the set of points in the plane. In Exercise 7 of the previous exercises the universal set could be either the set of natural numbers, or the set of integers. In calculus, the quantifiers usually refer to such universal sets as the set of real numbers, the set of positive real numbers, or the set of real functions.

Henceforth, we consider only nonempty universal sets. [The empty set is not very interesting to study.]

Definition. a) The sentence

$\forall x P(x)$

is true iff the solution set of P(x) equals the universal set (or, for every replacement of x by a member of the universal set u, P(u) is true).

b) The sentence

$\forall x P(x)$

is false iff the solution set of P(x) does not equal the universal set (or, there exists a replacement u in the universal set such that P(u) is false).

EXAMPLES.

Sentence $\forall x P(x)$	Universal Set	Solution Set of P(x)	Truth Value
$\forall x(x = 0)$	$\{0\}$	$\{0\}$	T
$\forall x(x = 0)$	$\{0, 1\}$	$\{0\}$	F
$\forall x(x < x + 1)$	R	R	T

$\forall x,\ 2x^2 + 3x + 1 = 0$	N	$\emptyset$	F
$\forall x,\ 2x^2 + 3x + 1 = 0$	$\bar{N}$	$\{-1\}$	F

EXERCISES

For each sentence of the type $\forall xP(x)$ and indicated universal set find the solution set of P(x), then the truth value of $\forall xP(x)$.

Sentence	Universal Set	Solution Set of P(x)	Truth Value
1. $\forall x,\ x < 0$	N		
2. $\forall x,\ x < 0$	I		
3. $\forall x,\ x < 0$	$\bar{N}$		
4. $\forall x,\ x^2 + 2x + 1 = 0$	R		
5. $\forall x,\ x + 0 = 0 + x = x$	R		
6. $\forall x,\ x^2 - 1 = (x-1)(x+1)$	R		

ANSWERS:

1. $\emptyset$; F
2. $\{\ldots, -3, -2, -1\}$; F
3. $\bar{N}$; T
4. $\{-1\}$; F
5. R; T
6. R; T

....

Definition. a) The sentence

$$\exists xP(x)$$

is true iff the solution set of P(x) is nonempty (or, there exists a replacement u such that P(u) is true).

b) The sentence

$$\exists xP(x)$$

is false iff the solution set of P(x) is empty (or, for every replacement of x by a member of the universal set u, P(u) is false).

EXAMPLES

Sentence $\exists xP(x)$	Universal Set	Solution Set of P(x)	Truth Value
$\exists x(x = 0)$	$\{0\}$	$\{0\}$	T
$\exists x(x = 0)$	$\{0, 1\}$	$\{0\}$	T
$\exists x,\ x < x + 1$	R	R	T
$\exists x,\ 2x^2 + 3x + 1 = 0$	N	$\emptyset$	F
$\exists x,\ 2x^2 + 3x + 1 = 0$	$\bar{N}$	$\{-1\}$	T

EXERCISES

For each sentence of the type $\exists xP(x)$ and indicated universal set find the solution set of $P(x)$, then the truth value of $\exists xP(x)$.

	Sentence	Universal Set	Solution Set of $P(x)$	Truth Value
1.	$\exists x,\ x < 0$	N		
2.	$\exists x,\ x < 0$	^{-}I		
3.	$\exists x,\ x < 0$	^{-}N		
4.	$\exists x,\ x^2 + 2x + 1 = 0$	R		
5.	$\exists x,\ x + 0 = 0 + x = x$	R		
6.	$\exists x,\ x^2 - 1 = (x-1)(x+1)$	R		

7. Compare truth values of the sentences $\forall xP(x)$ and $\exists xP(x)$ encountered in the previous examples and exercises. What can you conjecture about the truth value of $\exists x\, P(x)$ when $\forall x\, P(x)$ is true?

ANSWERS:

1. $\emptyset$; F
2. $\{\ldots, -3, -2, -1\}$; T
3. ^{-}N; T
4. $\{-1\}$; T
5. R; T
6. R; T
7. If $\forall xP(x)$ is true, then $\exists xP(x)$ is true. Recall that we are only considering <u>nonempty</u> universal sets. We will prove this later.

. . . .

TRUTH VALUES OF MORE COMPLICATED QUANTIFIED SENTENCES

<u>The sentence $\forall x \forall y P(x, y)$.</u> Suppose $P(x, y)$ is a sentence with two variables x and y. The sentence

$$\forall x \forall y\, P(x, y)$$

is true iff for every replacement of x and y by members a and b of the universal set,

$$P(a, b) \text{ is true.}$$

EXAMPLE. The sentence

$$\forall x \forall y,\ x + y = y + x$$

with universal set $\{0, 1, 2\}$ is true. Note that each of the following is true:

$0 + 1 = 1 + 0$	$1 + 2 = 2 + 1$	$2 + 2 = 2 + 2$
$1 + 0 = 0 + 1$	$2 + 1 = 1 + 2$	
$0 + 2 = 2 + 0$	$1 + 1 = 1 + 1$	
$2 + 0 = 0 + 2$		
$0 + 0 = 0 + 0$		

EXAMPLE. The sentence

$$\forall x \forall y,\ y < x$$

with universal set $\{0, 1, 2\}$ is false. When y is replaced by 2 and x by 1 the sentence

$$2 < 1$$

is false.

<u>The sentence $\exists x \exists y\ P(x, y)$.</u> The sentence

$$\exists x \exists y\ P(x, y)$$

is true iff there are replacements b for x and c for y such that

$$P(b, c) \text{ is true.}$$

EXAMPLE. The sentence

$$\exists x \exists y,\ x + 3 = 2 \cdot y$$

with universal set I is true. When x is replaced by 5 and y is replaced by 4, the sentence

$$5 + 3 = 2 \cdot 4$$

is true.

EXAMPLE. The sentence

$$\exists x \exists y,\ \frac{x}{y} = \sqrt{2}$$

with universal set I is false. There are no replacements of x and y by integers b and c which make the sentence

$$\frac{b}{c} = \sqrt{2}$$

true. We prove this later.

<u>The sentence $\forall x \exists y\ P(x, y)$.</u> The sentence

$$\forall x \exists y\ P(x, y)$$

is true iff for every replacement of x by a member of the universal set **b**,

$$\exists y\ P(b, y)$$

is true.

EXAMPLE. The sentence

$$\forall x \exists y,\ x + y = 0$$

with universal set $\{-1, 0, 1\}$ is true. Note:

$\exists y,\ 0 + y = 0$	(true; $y = 0$)
$\exists y,\ 1 + y = 0$	(true; $y = -1$)
$\exists y,\ -1 + y = 0$	(true; $y = 1$)

EXAMPLE. The sentence

$$\forall x \exists y,\ y < x$$

with universal set $\{0, 1, 2\}$ is false. Note:

$\exists y,\ y < 0$	(False; solution set of $y < 0$ is $\emptyset$)

$\exists y,\ y < 1$ (true; $y = 0$)
$\exists y,\ y < 2$ (true; $y = 0$, or 1)

The sentence $\exists y \forall x\ P(x, y)$. The sentence

$$\exists y \forall x\ P(x, y)$$

is true iff there exists a replacement c for y such that

$$\forall x\ P(x, c)$$

is true. Thus the same c makes the sentence

$$P(b, c)$$

true for every element b in the universal set.

EXAMPLE. The sentence

$$\exists y \forall x,\ x + y = x$$

with replacement set $\{0, 1, 2\}$ is true because the sentence

$$\forall x,\ x + 0 = x$$

is true.

EXAMPLE. The sentence

$$\exists y \forall x,\ y > x$$

with replacement set $\{0, 1, 2\}$ is false because each of the sentences

$$\forall x,\ 0 > x$$
$$\forall x,\ 1 > x$$
$$\forall x,\ 2 > x$$

is false; that is, there is no replacement b for y which makes the sentence

$$\forall x,\ b > x$$

true.

EXERCISES

Decide the truth value of each sentence with indicated universal set.

1. The universal set is $\{0, 1, 2\}$.

   a) $2 < 1 \rightarrow \exists x(x < 0)$
   b) $\forall x \exists y(y < x)$
   c) $\exists y \forall x(y < x)$
   d) $\exists y \forall x(y < x + 1)$
   e) $\forall x \exists y(y \leq x)$
   f) $\exists y \forall x(y \leq x)$
   g) $\forall x \exists y(x + y = 0)$
   h) $\forall x \forall y(x + y = y + x)$
   i) $\exists x \exists y,\ x + 5 = 2 + y$

2. The universal set is N. Answer (a) thru (i) above. Compare your answers to those of Exercise 1.
3. The universal set is I. Answer (a) thru (i) above. Compare your answers to those of Exercises 1 and 2.
4. The universal set is the set of all real functions.

a) $\forall f$ (f is differentiable)
b) $\forall f$ (f is differentiable $\rightarrow$ f is continuous)
c) $\exists f$ (f is continuous $\wedge$ f is differentiable)
d) $\exists f$ (f is continuous $\wedge$ f is not differentiable)

5. The universal set is the set of all infinite sequences $\{u_n\}$ of real numbers.
   a) $\forall \{u_n\}$ ($\Sigma |u_n|$ is convergent $\rightarrow$ Σu_n is convergent)
   b) $\forall \{u_n\}$, $\{u_n\}$ is convergent $\vee$ $\{u_n\}$ is divergent
   c) $\exists \{u_n\}$ ($\lim_{n\rightarrow\infty} u_n = 0 \wedge \Sigma u_n$ does not converge) Explain.
6. Consider the sentence $x < y$ with universal set I.
   a) Decide the truth value of $\forall x \exists y, x < y$
   b) Decide the truth value of $\exists y \forall x, x < y$
   c) Decide the truth value of $\forall x \exists y, x < y \rightarrow \exists y \forall x, x < y$
   d) Is every sentence of the type $\forall x \exists y \; P(x, y) \rightarrow \exists y \forall x \; P(x, y)$ true? Why?
   e) Decide the truth value of $\exists y \forall x, x < y \rightarrow \forall x \exists y, x < y$
   f) Use truth values for $\exists y \forall x \; P(x, y)$ and $\forall x \exists y \; P(x, y)$ in universal sets previously considered to compute truth values for
   $\exists y \forall x \; P(x, y) \rightarrow \forall x \exists y \; P(x, y)$.
   Does it seem that every sentence of the type
   $\exists y \forall x \; P(x, y) \rightarrow \forall x \exists y \; P(x, y)$ is true?

ANSWERS:

1. a) T
   b) F; the sentence $\exists y(y < 0)$ is false.
   c) F; each sentence $\forall x(0 < x)$, $\forall x(1 < x)$, $\forall x(2 < x)$ is false.
   d) T; $y = 0$
   e) T; Given an x there is a y, $y = x$, such that $y \leq x$.
   f) T; $\forall x(0 \leq x)$ is true.
   g) F; There is no number in the set which when added to 3 yields 0.
   h) T; this is the commutative law of addition.
   i) F
2. a) T b) F c) F d) T e) T
   f) F g) F h) T i) T
3. a) T b) T c) F d) F e) T
   f) F g) T h) T i) T
4. a) F; The function f described by $f(x) = |x|$ is not differentiable at 0 and hence not differentiable.
   b) T
   c) T; There are many such functions; e.g., $f(x) = \sin x$.
   d) T; See the answer to a.
5. a) T b) T c) T; $\Sigma u_n = \Sigma n^{-1}$
6. a) T b) F c) F d) No, "$x < y$" yields a false sentence of this type. See (c). e) T f) Yes, we prove this later.

Exercise 6 should have led you to see a distinction between the sentences

$$\forall x \exists y \ P(x, y)$$

and

$$\exists y \forall x \ P(x,y).$$

If the sentence

$\forall x \exists y \ P(x, y)$ is true

there is a dependence asserted between y and x. That is, the y depends on the x. If the sentence

$\exists y \forall x \ P(x, y)$ is true

there is no dependence of y on x. The same y makes P(x, y) true for all x.

Later we will prove that every sentence of the type

$$\exists y \forall x \ P(x, y) \rightarrow \forall x \exists y \ P(x, y)$$

is true.

EXERCISES

1. Let

   P(x): x is irrational
   Q(x): x is rational

   Decide the truth value of each of the following with universal set R.

   a) $\forall x[\ P(x) \vee Q(x)\ ]$
   b) $\forall x \ P(x)$
   c) $\forall x \ Q(x)$
   d) $\forall x \ P(x) \vee \forall x \ Q(x)$
   e) $\forall x[\ P(x) \vee Q(x)\ ] \rightarrow [\ \forall x \ P(x) \vee \forall x \ Q(x)\ ]$
   f) Is every sentence of the type
      $\forall x[\ P(x) \vee Q(x)\ ] \rightarrow [\ \forall x \ P(x) \vee \forall x \ Q(x)\ ]$ true?
2. By a procedure similar to Exercise 1 decide if every sentence of the type $[\exists x \ P(x) \wedge \exists x \ Q(x)\ ] \rightarrow \exists x[\ P(x) \wedge Q(x)\ ]$ is true.

ANSWERS:

1. a) T b) F c) F d) F e) F f) No
2. Every sentence of this type is not true.

....

REASONING SENTENCES

Mathematicians assume a certain class of sentences to be true before they ever prove any theorems in a mathematical system. We call these reasoning sentences or rules of reasoning. These rules are assumed by the mathematician, and accordingly could be called reasoning axioms.

Tautologies. An important class of these reasoning sentences are known as tautologies. A tautology is a sentence which is true no matter what the truth value of its constituent parts. [A review of truth tables for $\wedge$, $\vee$, $\sim$, $\rightarrow$, $\leftrightarrow$ would be helpful at this time.]

EXAMPLE. The sentence

$$P \rightarrow (P \vee Q)$$

is a tautology, where P and Q represent arbitrary mathematical sentences. We show this with a truth table. Truth values are obtained by successively breaking the sentence up into its constituent parts and computing truth values. Hence

P	Q	$P \vee Q$	$P \rightarrow (P \vee Q)$
T	T	T	T
T	F	T	T
F	T	T	T
F	F	F	T

Note that truth values for $P \vee Q$ were determined first and listed in column three. Then columns one and three were used to determine column four.

EXAMPLE. Show $(P \rightarrow Q) \leftrightarrow (\sim Q \rightarrow \sim P)$ is a tautology.

P	Q	$\sim P$	$\sim Q$	$P \rightarrow Q$	$\sim Q \rightarrow \sim P$	$(P \rightarrow Q) \leftrightarrow (\sim Q \rightarrow \sim P)$
T	T	F	F	T	T	T
T	F	F	T	F	F	T
F	T	T	F	T	T	T
F	F	T	T	T	T	T

Related to every conditional

$$P \rightarrow Q$$

is another conditional

$$\sim Q \rightarrow \sim P$$

called its contrapositive. We have just shown that the two are equivalent; that is, $(P \rightarrow Q) \leftrightarrow (\sim Q \rightarrow \sim P)$.

EXERCISES

Decide which of the following are tautologies.

1. $[P \wedge (P \rightarrow Q)] \rightarrow Q$ modus ponens
2. $[(P \rightarrow Q) \wedge (Q \rightarrow R)] \rightarrow (P \rightarrow R)$, Law of Syllogism, this truth table requires eight different combinations of truth values at the outset.
3. $\sim (P \wedge Q) \leftrightarrow (\sim P \vee \sim Q)$ } De Morgan's Laws
4. $\sim (P \vee Q) \leftrightarrow (\sim P \wedge \sim Q)$ }
5. $\sim (P \rightarrow Q) \leftrightarrow (P \wedge \sim Q)$

6. $(P \to Q) \leftrightarrow (\sim P \vee Q)$
7. $(P \wedge Q) \to P$
8. $\sim\sim P \leftrightarrow P$
9. $(P \wedge Q) \to (P \vee Q)$
10. $(P \to \sim Q) \to (Q \to \sim P)$
11. $(P \to Q) \to (Q \to P)$
12. $(P \vee Q) \to (P \wedge Q)$
13. $\sim P \to P$
14. $[(P \wedge R) \leftrightarrow (P \wedge Q)] \to (R \leftrightarrow Q)$
15. $[\sim P \wedge (R \wedge \sim R)] \to P$ } Proof by Contradiction
16. $[(P \wedge \sim Q) \wedge (R \wedge \sim R)] \to (P \to Q)$
17. $P \vee \sim P$

ANSWERS:

1 - 10, 15, 16, 17 are tautologies. 11 - 14 are not.

. . . .

Other Tautologies. The tautologies in the previous exercises are quite useful. Below are several other useful tautologies.

$P \leftrightarrow P$

$P \to P$

$[P \to (Q \vee R)] \to [(P \wedge \sim Q) \to R]$

$[(P \to S_1) \wedge (S_1 \to S_2) \wedge \ldots \wedge (S_{n-1} \to S_n) \wedge (S_n \to R)] \to [P \to R]$
Law of Syllogism

$[(P \to R) \wedge (Q \to R)] \to [(P \vee Q) \to R]$ Proof by Cases

$(P \wedge Q) \leftrightarrow (Q \wedge P)$ } Commutative Laws
$(P \vee Q) \leftrightarrow (Q \vee P)$

$[P \to (R \to Q)] \leftrightarrow [(P \wedge R) \to Q]$

$[P \wedge (Q \wedge R)] \leftrightarrow [(P \wedge Q) \wedge R]$ } Associative Laws
$[P \vee (Q \vee R)] \leftrightarrow [(P \vee Q) \vee R]$

$[P \wedge (Q \vee R)] \leftrightarrow [(P \wedge Q) \vee (P \wedge R)]$ } Distributive Laws
$[P \vee (Q \wedge R)] \leftrightarrow [(P \vee Q) \wedge (P \vee R)]$

$[(P \leftrightarrow Q_1) \wedge \ldots \wedge (Q_n \leftrightarrow Q)] \to (P \leftrightarrow Q)$

This list is not exhaustive. If you want to make a deduction based on a sentence, check its truth table. If it is a tautology use it. Tautologies provide lots of reasoning theorems before we ever start deduction within a mathematical system.

VALID ARGUMENTS

An argument is an assertion that from a certain set of sentences $S_1, \ldots, S_n$ (called premises or assumptions) one can deduce another sentence Q (called a conclusion or inference). Such an argument will be denoted

$$S_1, \ldots, S_n \vdash Q.$$

Arguments are either valid (correct) or invalid (incorrect).

The following is a valid argument.

<u>Rule of Modus Ponens.</u> From any conditional $P \to Q$ and also P, one may conclude Q; that is P, $P \to Q$, therefore Q. This is a valid argument and can be denoted two ways.

a) $P,\ P \to Q \vdash Q$

b)
$$\begin{array}{l} P \to Q \\ \underline{P\qquad\quad} \\ \therefore Q \end{array}$$

This rule is based on the tautology

$$[P \wedge (P \to Q)] \to Q,$$

for if you check its truth table you see that when P is true and $P \to Q$ is true, then Q must be true.

When using modus ponens the form of the sentence is important.

1. (   ) → [   ]
2. (   )
3. ∴ [   ]

Having placed sentences in the parentheses (the same sentence must be in both sets of parentheses) and the brackets, and assuming sentences 1 and 2 true, we deduce sentence 3.

EXAMPLE. If $f(x) = \sin x$, then $f'(x) = \cos x$
$f(x) = \sin x$
$\therefore f'(x) = \cos x$

EXAMPLE. $x = 5$ only if $2x = 10$
$x = 5$
$\therefore 2x = 10$

EXERCISE

Complete.

$3x = 15$ if $x = 5$
$x = 5$
∴ ________

ANSWERS:

$3x = 15$

....

<u>Rule of Subsititution.</u> Suppose $P \leftrightarrow Q$. Then P and Q may be substituted for one another in any sentence.

EXAMPLE. $P \leftrightarrow Q$
$R \to (S \wedge Q)$
$\therefore R \to (S \wedge P)$

You may insert a tautology into any set of premises.

EXAMPLE. $P \to Q$ premise
$(P \to Q) \to (\sim Q \to \sim P)$ tautology
$\therefore \sim Q \to \sim P$

EXERCISES

Complete.

1. $P, P \leftrightarrow Q \vdash$ ________

2. P premise
   $P \to$ (______) tautology

   $\therefore P \vee Q$

ANSWER:

1. Q   2. $P \vee Q$

....

EXAMPLE. Deduce $\sim P$ from the premises $\sim Q$ and $P \to Q$.

1. $\sim Q$ } premises
2. $P \to Q$
3. $(P \to Q) \to (\sim Q \to \sim P)$ tautology

$\therefore$ 4. $\sim Q \to \sim P$, by modus ponens on 2 and 3

1. $\sim Q$
4. $\sim Q \to \sim P$

$\therefore$ 5. $\sim P$, by modus ponens

EXAMPLE. Deduce S from the premises $\sim S \to H$, $H \to \sim I$, and I.

1. $\sim S \to H$ } premises
2. $H \to \sim I$
3. I
4. $(H \to \sim I) \to (I \to \sim H)$ tautology

$\therefore$ 5. $I \to \sim H$, by modus ponens on 2 and 4

5. $I \to \sim H$
3. I

$\therefore$ 6. $\sim H$, by modus ponens

1. $\sim S \to H$
7. $(\sim S \to H) \to (\sim H \to S)$ tautology

$\therefore$ 8. $\sim H \to S$, by modus ponens

8. $\sim H \to S$
6. $\sim H$

$\therefore$ S, by modus ponens

Another way to show that $S_1, \ldots, S_n \vdash Q$ is a valid argument is to show that $(S_1 \wedge \ldots \wedge S_n) \to Q$ is a tautology.

EXAMPLE. $P, P \to Q \vdash Q$ is valid because $[P \wedge (P \to Q)] \to Q$ is a tautology.

EXAMPLE. $Q, P \to Q \vdash P$ is <u>not</u> a valid argument because $[Q \wedge (P \to Q)] \to P$ is not a tautology. [Such an inference might be referred to as "modus humorous".]

EXERCISES

Determine the validity of each of the following.

1. $\sim (P \rightarrow Q) \vdash P$
2. $\sim P \wedge \sim Q \vdash \sim P$
3. $P \rightarrow (Q \vee R),\ P \wedge \sim Q \vdash R$
4. $(P \wedge R) \rightarrow Q,\ P \wedge R \vdash Q$
5. $\sim P,\ P \vee Q \vdash Q$
6. $P \rightarrow R,\ Q \rightarrow P,\ \sim R \vdash \sim Q$
7. $P \rightarrow Q,\ R \rightarrow \sim Q \vdash R \rightarrow \sim P$
8. $P \vee Q \vdash Q$
9. $P \rightarrow Q \vdash Q \rightarrow P$ ($Q \rightarrow P$ is the <u>converse</u> of $P \rightarrow Q$)
10. $P \wedge Q \vdash P \vee Q$
11. $P \vee Q \vdash P \wedge Q$

ANSWERS:

1. Valid	2. Valid	3. Valid	4. Valid
5. Valid	6. Valid	7. Valid	8. Invalid
9. Invalid	10. Valid	11. Invalid	

....

CONTRAPOSITIVES

Recall that the contrapositive of $P \rightarrow Q$ is $\sim Q \rightarrow \sim P$. The two sentences are equivalent. Contrapositives reveal added insight.

EXAMPLES. In calculus the sentence

$$\text{"If } \sum_{n=1}^{\infty} u_n \text{ converges, then } \lim_{n\to\infty} u_n = 0\text{"}$$

is true. If we translate the sentence

$$P: \sum_{n=1}^{\infty} u_n \text{ converges}$$

$$Q: \lim_{n\to\infty} u_n = 0$$

then $P \rightarrow Q$ is true. Its contrapositive is also true because $(P \rightarrow Q) \leftrightarrow (\sim Q \rightarrow \sim P)$ is a tautology and, by the rule of substitution, $\sim Q \rightarrow \sim P$ is true. That is,

$$\text{"If } \lim_{n\to\infty} u_n \neq 0, \text{ then } \sum_{n=1}^{\infty} u_n \text{ diverges"}$$

is true. Recall that to check the convergence of a series you determine if the n'th term converges to 0. If it does not, you know the series cannot converge.

EXAMPLE. The sentence

$$"\sum_{n=1}^{\infty} |u_n| \text{ converges} \rightarrow \sum_{n=1}^{\infty} u_n \text{ converges}"$$

is true; that is,

"If a series is absolutely convergent, then it is convergent"

is true. Its contrapositive is also true because

$$\left(\sum_{n=1}^{\infty} |u_n| \text{ conv.} \rightarrow \sum_{n=1}^{\infty} u_n \text{ conv.}\right) \leftrightarrow \left(\sum_{n=1}^{\infty} u_n \text{ div} \rightarrow \sum_{n=1}^{\infty} |u_n| \text{ div.}\right)$$

by tautology. Then by the rule of substitution we have

$$"\sum_{n=1}^{\infty} u_n \text{ div.} \rightarrow \sum_{n=1}^{\infty} |u_n| \text{ div."}$$

In summary, a conditional is true iff its contrapositive is true.

EXERCISES

1. Form the contrapositive of the sentence "If $f(x) = \sin x$, then $f'(x) = \cos x$." Is this new sentence true? Why?

Form the contrapositive of the following. Use $\rightarrow$.

2. x is odd is a necessary condition for x not being even.
3. x is rational is a sufficient condition for x to be real.
4. If f is differentiable, then f is continuous.
5. $x \in A \rightarrow x \in B$
6. x^2 odd $\rightarrow$ x odd
7. x^2 even $\rightarrow$ x even
8. x is even only if x^2 is even
9. $A \cap B \neq \emptyset \rightarrow A \neq \emptyset$
10. $[\forall e(|x| < e)] \rightarrow x = 0$
11. $f(x) = f(y) \rightarrow x = y$
12. $x \leq y \rightarrow f(x) \leq f(y)$
13. $x < y \rightarrow f(x) < f(y)$

ANSWERS:

1. If $f'(x) \neq \cos x$, then $f(x) \neq \sin x$. Yes, because the previous sentence is true and its contrapositive is equivalent to it.
2. x is not odd $\rightarrow$ x is even.

3. x is not real $\rightarrow$ x is not rational.
4. f discontinuous $\rightarrow$ f is not differentiable.
5. $x \notin B \rightarrow x \notin A$
6. x even $\rightarrow$ x^2 even
7. x odd $\rightarrow$ x^2 odd
8. x^2 odd $\rightarrow$ x odd
9. $A = \emptyset \rightarrow A \cap B = \emptyset$
10. $x \neq 0 \rightarrow \sim \forall e(|x| < e)$
11. $x \neq y \rightarrow f(x) \neq f(y)$
12. $f(x) > f(y) \rightarrow x > y$
13. $f(x) \geq f(y) \rightarrow x \geq y$

NEGATIONS

Negations of $\forall xP(x)$ and $\exists xP(x)$. It is often useful to express the negations of sentences of the type $\forall x\ P(x)$ and $\exists x\ P(x)$ in other forms.

Theorem 1. Every sentence of the type

$$\sim \forall x\, P(x) \leftrightarrow \exists x \sim P(x)$$

is true.

Proof. We prove that $\sim \forall x\, P(x)$ and $\exists x \sim P(x)$ are equivalent by showing that their truth values agree.

Suppose $\sim \forall x\, P(x)$ is true. Then $\forall x\, P(x)$ is false so there exists a replacement u in the universal set such that

P(u) is false.

Then

$\sim$ P(u) is true

for this replacement u. Thus,

$\exists x \sim P(x)$ is true.

Suppose $\sim \forall x\, P(x)$ is false. Then $\forall x\, P(x)$ is true, so for every replacement u

P(u) is true

Hence, for every replacement u,

$\sim$ P(u) is false

Thus

$\exists x \sim P(x)$ is false.

Therefore, $\sim \forall x\, P(x)$ and $\exists x \sim P(x)$ are equivalent.

EXERCISE

Apply the tautology $(P \leftrightarrow Q) \leftrightarrow (\sim P \leftrightarrow \sim Q)$ to the previous theorem to complete the following

$\forall x\, P(x) \leftrightarrow$ ________________

ANSWER:

$\sim \exists x \sim P(x)$

....

You have proved the following theorem.

Theorem 2. Every sentence of the type

$\forall x\, P(x) \leftrightarrow \sim \exists x \sim P(x)$

is true.

Using Theorems 1 and 2 we can prove the following theorem.

Theorem 3. Every sentence of the type

$\sim \exists x\, P(x) \leftrightarrow \forall x \sim P(x)$

is true.

Proof. $\sim\ x \sim P(x) \leftrightarrow \exists x \sim\sim P(x)$ by Theorem 1 where we substitute $\sim P(x)$ for $P(x)$. Now by tautology we know $\sim\sim P(x) \leftrightarrow P(x)$. Hence $\exists x \sim\sim P(x) \leftrightarrow \exists x\, P(x)$. Thus we have $\sim \forall x \sim P(x) \leftrightarrow \exists x\, P(x)$ by the Rule of Substitution.

EXERCISE

Prove the following theorem.

Theorem 4. Every sentence of the type

$\exists x\, P(x) \leftrightarrow \sim \forall x \sim P(x)$

is true.

ANSWER:

Proof. We know

$\sim \exists x\, P(x) \leftrightarrow \forall x \sim P(x)$

then

$\sim\sim \exists x\, P(x) \leftrightarrow \sim \forall x \sim P(x)$

or

$\exists x\, P(x) \leftrightarrow \sim \forall x \sim P(x)$

....

We have established the rules:

1) $\sim \forall x P(x) \leftrightarrow \exists x \sim P(x)$
2) $\forall x P(x) \leftrightarrow \sim \exists x \sim P(x)$
3) $\sim \exists x P(x) \leftrightarrow \forall x \sim P(x)$

4) $\exists x P(x) \leftrightarrow \sim \forall x \sim P(x)$

The usefulness of these rules will be realized when doing proofs by contrapositive and by contradiction.

Simplified Negations. Moving the negation symbol past the quantifiers of a sentence provides a more meaningful, simplified, translation of the negation.

EXAMPLE. A simplified negation of

$$\forall x \forall y \exists z(x + y = z)$$

is

$$\exists x \exists y \forall z(x + y \neq z)$$

To show this notice that

$$\begin{aligned} \sim \forall x \forall y \exists z(x + y = z) &\leftrightarrow \exists x \sim \forall y \exists z(x + y = z), \text{ by rule (1)} \\ &\leftrightarrow \exists x \exists y \sim \exists z(x + y = z), \text{ by rule (1)} \\ &\leftrightarrow \exists x \exists y \forall z \sim (x + y = z), \text{ by rule (3)} \\ &\leftrightarrow \exists x \exists y \forall z(x + y \neq z), \text{ by substituting } xy \neq z \\ &\quad \text{for } \sim (x + y = z) \end{aligned}$$

EXAMPLE. A simplified negation of

$$\exists y \forall x(xy \leq 2)$$

is

$$\forall y \exists x(xy > 2)$$

To show this notice that

$$\begin{aligned} \sim \exists y \forall x(xy \leq 2) &\leftrightarrow \forall y \sim \forall x(xy \leq 2), \text{ by (3)} \\ &\leftrightarrow \forall y \exists x \sim (xy \leq 2), \text{ by (1)} \\ &\leftrightarrow \forall y \exists x(xy > 2), \text{ by substituting } xy > 2 \text{ for} \\ &\qquad \sim (xy \leq 2) \end{aligned}$$

Perhaps you have discovered that forming a simplified negation which begins with a series of quantifiers amounts to changing each existential quantifier to a universal quantifier and vice versa and moving the negation symbol to the right of the quantifiers.

EXAMPLE. A simplified negation of

$$\forall x \exists y \forall z(xy = z)$$

is

$$\exists x \forall y \exists z(xy \neq z)$$

EXERCISE

Form a negation of $\forall x \forall y \forall z \exists q \exists j(xyzq = j)$

ANSWER:

$\exists x \exists y \exists z \forall q \forall j(xyzq \neq j)$

Further simplifications of negations can be formed using tautologies.

EXAMPLE. A simplified negation of

$$\forall x[\, P(x) \vee Q(x)\,]$$

is

$$\exists x[\sim P(x) \wedge \sim Q(x)\,]$$

Now

$$\begin{aligned} \sim \forall x[\, P(x) \vee Q(x)\,] &\leftrightarrow \exists x \sim[\, P(x) \vee Q(x)\,], \text{ by (1)} \\ &\leftrightarrow \exists x[\sim P(x) \vee \sim Q(x)\,], \text{ by the tautology} \\ &\qquad \sim (P \wedge Q) \leftrightarrow (\sim P \vee \sim Q) \end{aligned}$$

EXAMPLE. A simplified negation of

$$\exists x[\, P(x) \rightarrow Q(x)\,]$$

is

$$\forall x[\, P(x) \wedge \sim Q(x)\,]$$

Now

$$\begin{aligned} \sim \exists x[\, P(x) \rightarrow Q(x)\,] &\leftrightarrow \forall x \sim[\, P(x) \rightarrow Q(x)\,], \text{ by (3)} \\ &\leftrightarrow \forall x[\, P(x) \wedge \sim Q(x)\,], \text{ by the tautology} \\ &\qquad \sim (P \rightarrow Q) \leftrightarrow (P \wedge \sim Q) \end{aligned}$$

EXAMPLE. A simplified negation of

$$\forall x\, \exists y[\, P(x) \wedge y \leq x\,]$$

is

$$\exists x\, \forall y[\sim P(x) \vee y > x\,]$$

Now

$$\begin{aligned} \sim \forall x \exists y[\, P(x) \wedge y \leq x\,] &\leftrightarrow \exists x \forall y \sim[\, P(x) \wedge y \leq x\,] \\ &\leftrightarrow \exists x \forall y[\sim P(x) \wedge y > x\,], \text{ by the tautology} \\ &\qquad \sim (P \wedge Q) \leftrightarrow (\sim P \vee \sim Q) \end{aligned}$$

EXERCISE

Form a simplified negation of $\exists x\, \forall y[\, y < x \rightarrow P(x)\,]$

ANSWER:

$\forall x\, \exists y[\, y < x \wedge \sim P(x)\,]$

....

<u>More on the Utility of Negations.</u> Quantifiers within the same sentence can refer to different universal sets. The universal sets can be described within the sentence; for example,

$$\forall n \in N\ \exists x > 0(n^2 > x)$$

refers to N   refers to the positive real numbers

The rules for negation still holds; that is

$$\sim \forall n \in N \exists x > 0 (n^2 > x) \leftrightarrow \exists n \in N \forall x > 0 (n^2 \leq x).$$

Suppose we have a complicated sentence as in the following definition.

Definition. A is the limit of the sequence $\{a_n\}_{n=1}^{\infty}$ iff for each $\epsilon > 0$ there exists a natural number m such that for every $n > m$, $|a_n - A| < \epsilon$.

EXERCISES

1. Translate the previous definition to logical symbolism.

   A is the limit of $\{a_n\}_{n=1}^{\infty}$ $\leftrightarrow$ ______________________________.

2. Form a simplified negation of the sentence.

   A is not the limit of $\{a_n\}_{n=1}^{\infty}$ $\leftrightarrow$ ______________________________.

ANSWERS:

1. $\forall \epsilon > 0 \exists m \in N \forall n > m, |a_n - A| < \epsilon$
2. $\exists \epsilon > 0 \forall m \in N \exists n > m, |a_n - A| \geq \epsilon$

. . . .

Now if we wanted to prove that A is not the limit of $\{a_n\}_{n=1}^{\infty}$ we know what we must show.

A knowledge of logic helped in three ways:

1) It helped translate a complicated sentence into more meaningful symbolism.
2) It enabled us to find a negation of the sentence.
3) With this negation we knew what had to be shown to prove the first sentence false.

As another example consider the definition of an increasing function.

Definition. A function f is increasing iff for every x and for every y; if $x \leq y$, then $f(x) \leq f(y)$.

EXERCISES

1. Translate the previous definition to logical symbolism. A function f is increasing $\leftrightarrow$ ________________________.
2. Form a simplified negation of the sentence A function f is not increasing $\leftrightarrow$ ________________________.

ANSWERS:

1. $\forall x \forall y [x \leq y \rightarrow f(x) \leq f(y)]$
2. $\exists x \exists y [x \leq y \wedge f(x) > f(y)]$

. . . .

EXAMPLE. The function $f(x) = x^2$ is not increasing. When $x = -2$ and $y = 1$,

$$x \le y,$$
$$f(x) = 4,$$
$$f(y) = 1$$

and

$$f(x) > f(y)$$

<u>Counterexamples.</u> To prove a sentence of the type

$$\forall x\, P(x)$$

false one could try to prove

$$\exists x \sim P(x)$$

true. This is referred to as "providing a counterexample".

EXERCISES

Consider the sentence

$$\forall x,\ x^2 = x$$

with universal set R

1. Form a simplified negation of the sentence. ____________________.
2. Prove the negation true.

ANSWERS:

1. $\exists x,\ x^2 \neq x$
2. Let $x = 2$. Then $x^2 = 4$ so $x^2 \neq x$.

....

EXERCISES

Form a simplified negation.

1. $\exists x,\ x < 0 \wedge Q(x)$.
2. $\forall x \exists y \forall z \forall q \exists j,\ x + y + z + q + j = 0$
3. $(P \wedge \sim Q) \rightarrow \sim R$
4. $\sim \forall x \forall y \exists z,\ xz = y$
5. $\forall e \exists d \forall x [\ |x - c| < d \rightarrow |f(x) - f(c)| < e]$
6. $\forall e \exists n \forall m [\ m > n \rightarrow |a_m - a| < e]$
7. $(x \in Q \wedge y \in J) \rightarrow x + y \in J$
8. $(P \wedge Q) \rightarrow R$
9. $x \in A \wedge x \in B$
10. $x \in A \vee x \in B$
11. $(P_1 \wedge \ldots \wedge P_n) \rightarrow Q$
12. $P \leftrightarrow Q$

For each of 13-28

a) express in logical symbolism, and

b) express simplified negations in logical symbolism.

13. The Archimedean Property. For every two positive real numbers a and b there exists an $n \in N$ such that $na > b$.
14. A function f is even iff for every x, $f(-x) = f(x)$.
15. A function f is odd iff for every x, $f(-x) = -f(x)$.
16. A function f is constant iff for every x and for every y, $f(x) = f(y)$
17. A function f is periodic iff there exists a $p > 0$ such that for every x, $f(x + p) = f(x)$.
18. A function f is decreasing iff for every x and for every y: if $x \leq y$, then $f(x) \geq f(y)$.
19. A function f is strictly increasing iff for every x and for every y; if $x < y$, then $f(x) < f(y)$.
20. A function f is strictly decreasing iff for every x and for every y; if $x < y$, then $f(x) > f(y)$.
21. A function f is one-to-one iff for every x and for every y; if $f(x) = f(y)$, then $x = y$.
22. A function $f : A \to B$ is onto iff for every $y \in B$ there exists an $x \in A$ such that $f(x) = y$.
23. A function f has a limit L at x_o iff for every x and for every $\epsilon > 0$, there exists a $\delta > 0$ such that $|f(x) - L| < \epsilon$ whenever $0 < |x - x_o| < \delta$.
24. A function f is bounded iff there exists an M such that for every x, $|f(x)| \leq M$.
25. A function f is continuous at x_o iff for every x and for every $\epsilon > 0$ there is a $\delta > 0$ such that if $|x - x_o| < \delta$, then $|f(x)-f(x_o)| < \epsilon$.
26. A function f is continuous on a set E iff for any x in E and any $\epsilon > 0$, there exists a $\delta > 0$ such that $|f(x) - f(y)| < \epsilon$ whenever y is in E and $|x - y| < \delta$.
27. A function f is uniformly continuous on a set E iff for any $\epsilon > 0$, there exists a $\delta > 0$ such that $|f(x) - f(y)|$ whenever x and y are in E and $|x - y| \leq \delta$.
28. A sequence $\{a_n\}_{n=1}^{\infty}$ is Cauchy iff for every $\epsilon > 0$, there exists a positive integer n_o such that $|a_n - a_m| < \epsilon$ whenever m and n are greater than n_o.

Find counterexamples for each of the following.

29. $\forall \{u_n\}_{n=1}^{\infty} [\sum_{n=1}^{\infty} u_n$ converges$]$

30. $\forall \{u_n\}_{n=1}^{\infty} [\lim_{n\to\infty} u_n = 0 \to \sum_{n=1}^{\infty} u_n$ converges$]$

31. $\forall f$ (f is continuous $\to f$ is differentiable)

32. $\forall f$, f is bounded

ANSWERS:

1. $\forall x, x \geq 0 \wedge \sim Q(x)$
2. $\exists x \forall y \exists z \exists q \forall j, x + y + z + q + j \neq 0$
3. $P \wedge \sim Q \wedge R$
4. $\forall x \forall y \exists z, xz = y$
5. $\exists e \forall d \exists x [\, |x-c| < d \wedge |f(x) - f(c)| \geq e]$
6. $\exists e \forall n \exists m [\, m > n \wedge |a_m - a| \geq e]$
7. $x \in Q \wedge x \in J \wedge x + y \notin J$ or $x \in Q \wedge x \in J \wedge x + y \in Q$
8. $P \wedge Q \wedge \sim R$
9. $x \notin A \vee x \notin B$
10. $x \notin A \wedge x \notin B$
11. $P_1 \wedge \ldots \wedge P_n \wedge \sim Q$
12. $(P \wedge \sim Q) \vee (Q \wedge \sim P)$
13. a) $\forall a > 0 \forall b > 0 \exists n \in N, na > b$

    b) $\exists a > 0 \exists b > 0 \forall n \in N, na \leq b$
14. a) $\forall x, f(-x) = f(x)$

    b) $\exists x, f(-x) \neq f(x)$
15. a) $\forall x, f(-x) = -f(x)$

    b) $\exists x, f(-x) \neq -f(x)$
16. a) $\forall x \forall y, f(x) = f(y)$

    b) $\exists x \exists y, f(x) \neq f(y)$
17. a) $\exists p > 0 \forall x, f(x + p) = f(x)$

    b) $\forall p > 0 \exists x, f(x + p) \neq f(x)$
18. a) $\forall x \forall y [\, x \leq y \to f(x) \geq f(y)]$

    b) $\exists x \exists y [\, x \leq y \wedge f(x) < f(y)]$
19. a) $\forall x \forall y [\, x < y \to f(x) < f(y)]$

    b) $\exists x \exists y [\, x < y \wedge f(x) \geq f(y)]$
20. a) $\forall x \forall y [\, x < y \to f(x) > f(y)]$

    b) $\exists x \exists y [\, x < y \wedge f(x) \leq f(y)]$
21. a) $\forall x \forall y [\, f(x) = f(y) \to x = y]$

    b) $\exists x \exists y [\, f(x) = f(y) \wedge x \neq y]$
22. a) $\forall y \in B \exists x \in A, f(x) = y$

    b) $\exists y \in B \forall x \in A, f(x) \neq y$
23. a) $\forall x \forall \epsilon > 0 \exists \delta > 0, 0 < |x - x_o| < \delta \to |f(x) - L| < \epsilon$

    b) $\exists x \exists \epsilon > 0 \forall \delta > 0, 0 < |x - x_o| < \delta \wedge |f(x) - L| \geq \epsilon$
24. a) $\exists M \forall x, |f(x)| \leq M$

    b) $\forall M \exists x, |f(x)| > M$
25. a) $\forall x \forall \epsilon > 0 \exists \delta > 0, |x - x_o| < \delta \to |f(x) - f(x_o)| < \epsilon$

    b) $\exists x \exists \epsilon > 0 \forall \delta > 0, |x - x_o| < \delta \wedge |f(x) - f(x_o)| \geq \epsilon$
26. a) $\forall x \in E \forall \epsilon > 0 \exists \delta > 0 \forall y \in E, |x - y| < \delta \to |f(x) - f(y)| < \epsilon$

b) $\exists x \in E \; \exists \epsilon > 0 \forall \delta > 0 \exists y \in E, \; |x - y| < \delta \wedge |f(x) - f(y)| \geq \epsilon$

27. a) $\forall \epsilon > 0 \exists \delta > 0 \forall x \in E \; \forall y \in E, \; |x - y| < \delta \rightarrow |f(x) - f(y)| < \epsilon$

b) $\exists \epsilon > 0 \forall \delta > 0 \exists x \in E \; \exists y \in E, \; |x - y| < \delta \wedge |f(x) - f(y)| \geq \epsilon$

28. a) $\forall \epsilon > 0 \exists n_o \in N \forall m \in n \; \forall n \in n, (m > n_o \wedge n > n_o) \rightarrow |a_n - a_m| < \epsilon$

b) $\exists \epsilon > 0 \forall n_o \in N \exists m \in n \exists n \in n, (m > n_o \wedge n > n_o) \wedge |a_n - a_m| \geq \epsilon$

29. $\sum_{n=1}^{\infty} n^{-1}$ does not converge.

30. To show: $\exists \{u_n\}_{n=1}^{\infty}, \lim_{n\to\infty} u_n = 0 \wedge \sum_{n=1}^{\infty} u_n$ does not converge.

Consider $\{n^{-1}\}_{n=1}^{\infty}; \lim_{n\to\infty} n^{-1} = 0 \wedge \sum_{n=1}^{\infty} n^{-1}$ does not converge.

31. $f(x) = |x|$ provides a counterexample.

32. $f(x) = x^2$ provides a counterexample.

. . . .

It is time for a test. Do the following:

1) Review all the material giving special emphasis to such concepts as sets, truth tables, tautologies, validity, and so on.
2) Be able to translate a sentence into logical symbolism and form simplified negations.
3) Study a day or two before taking the test.

Take the test only after a careful review. The purpose of the test is to decide if you have learned the previous material sufficiently to proceed with subsequent material. If you are studying this book as part of a course given by an instructor, the test will evaluate your learning and assist you in preparing for a possible classroom test.

Having completed your preparation, turn to the next page and take the test. Do not refer to the text or to your notes. You should be able to complete the test in one hour, but take all the time you need. Having completed the test, use the answer key and carry out the analysis on the page entitled "Test 1 - Analysis".

TEST 1

---

1. If a universal set U = { 1, 2, 3, 4, 5 } , A = { 1, 4, 5 } , and B = { 4,5 } , find:

   a) $A \cup B$ = ________

   b) $A \cap B$ = ________

   c) $\complement A$ = ________

   d) Is $B \subset A$? ______

2. Give the truth value.

   ______ a) $\sim (2 < 3 \rightarrow 1 > 2)$

   ______ b) $\sim$ (e is real $\vee$ e is an integer)

   ______ c) 2 is even $\leftrightarrow$ 2 is prime

   ______ d) $(1 - \frac{1}{2} + \frac{1}{3} - \frac{1}{4} + \ldots)$ is convergent $\rightarrow$ $(1 + \frac{1}{2} + \frac{1}{3} + \frac{1}{4} + \ldots)$ is convergent

3. a) Complete this truth table

P	Q	$\sim P$	$P \wedge \sim P$	$(P \wedge \sim P) \rightarrow Q$
T	T			
T	F			
F	T			
F	F			

   b) Is $(P \wedge \sim P) \rightarrow Q$ a tautology? ________

4. a) Complete this truth table:

P	Q	$P \vee Q$	$(P \vee Q) \rightarrow P$
T	T		
T	F		
F	T		
F	F		

b) Is $(P \vee Q) \rightarrow P$ a tautology? ________

5. Give the truth value of each sentence relative to each universal set.

		I	{3}
a)	$\forall x \exists y(x + y = 0)$		
b)	$\exists y \forall x(x + y = 0)$		

6. The contrapositive of $P \rightarrow Q$ is

a) $P \rightarrow \sim Q$

b) $Q \rightarrow P$

c) $\sim Q \rightarrow \sim P$

d) Q

7. Determine the validity of each.

a) $P,\ P \rightarrow Q \quad Q$

b) $Q,\ P \rightarrow Q \quad P$

8. Translate using $\sim$, $\wedge$, $\vee$, $\rightarrow$, $\leftrightarrow$, $\exists$, $\forall$, and the following symbols for sentences.

N(x): x is a natural number
I(x): x is an integer
E(x): x is even
D(x): x is odd
Q(x): x is rational
R(x): x is real
P(x): x is prime
x=2: x is equal to 2

a) All natural numbers are real numbers. ________________

b) Some real numbers are not rational. ________________

c) There exists an integer that is even and prime. ________________

d) All rational numbers are real numbers. ________________

e) Not all real numbers are rational. ________________

f) All prime numbers are odd except 2. ________________

g) Every integer is odd or even. ____________

h) x is rational only if x is real. ____________

i) x is an integer is a sufficient condition for x being a rational number. ____________

j) x is odd is a necessary condition for x not being even. ________

k) x is an integer is a necessary and sufficient condition for x being odd or even. ____________

l) x is prime and x is even if and only if x equals 2. ____________

9. A negation of

"For every x, x is even"

is

a) For every x, x is odd
b) There exists an x such that x is odd
c) For every x, x is even
d) There exists an x such that x is even
e) None of the above

10. A negation of

"There exists some function f which is continuous"

is

a) There is some f which is not continuous
b) For every f, f is not continuous
c) There is an f which is continuous
d) For every f, f is continuous
e) None of the above

11. A negation of

$$\forall e \exists m \forall n [n \geq m \rightarrow |a_n - a| < e]$$

is

a) $\exists e \forall m \exists n [n \geq m \wedge |a_n - a| \geq e]$
b) $\exists e \forall m \exists n [n \geq m \rightarrow |a_n - a| \geq e]$
c) $\forall e \exists m \forall n [n \geq m \wedge |a_n - a| \geq e]$

d) $\forall e \exists m \forall n [n \geq m \rightarrow | a_n - a | \geq e]$

e) $\exists e \forall m \exists n [| a_n - a | \geq e \rightarrow n < m]$

KEY:

1. (2 pts. each)
   a) A b) B c) $\{2, 3\}$ d) Yes
2. (2 pts. each)
   a) T b) F c) T d) F
3. a) (6 pts.)

$\sim P$	$P \wedge \sim P$	$(P \wedge \sim P) \rightarrow Q$
F	F	T
F	F	T
T	F	T
T	F	T

   b) (2 pts.) Yes
4. a) (6 pts.)

$P \vee Q$	$(P \vee Q) \rightarrow P$
T	T
T	T
T	F
F	T

   b) (2 pts.) No
5. (2 pts. each)
   a) T, F b) F, F
6. (4 pts.) C
7. (4 pts. each)
   a) Valid b) Invalid
8. (3 pts. each)
   a) $\forall x,\ N(x) \rightarrow R(x)$
   b) $\exists x,\ R(x) \wedge \sim Q(x)$
   c) $\exists x,\ N(x) \wedge E(x) \wedge P(x)$
   d) $\forall x,\ Q(x) \rightarrow R(x)$
   e) $\sim [\forall x, R(x) \rightarrow Q(x)]$, or $\exists x \sim [R(x) \rightarrow Q(x)]$, or $\exists x,\ R(x) \wedge \sim Q(x)$
   f) $\forall x, (P(x) \wedge x \neq 2) \rightarrow D(x)$, or $\forall x,\ P(x) \rightarrow [D(x) \vee x = 2]$
   g) $\forall x,\ I(x) \rightarrow [D(x) \vee E(x)]$
   h) $Q(x) \rightarrow R(x)$
   i) $I(x) \rightarrow Q(x)$
   j) $\sim E(x) \rightarrow D(x)$
   k) $I(x) \leftrightarrow [D(x) \vee E(x)]$
   l) $[P(x) \wedge E(x)] \leftrightarrow x = 2$
9. (4 pts.) b
10. (4 pts.) b
11. (4 pts.) a

TEST 1 - ANALYSIS

The test key shows the number of points for each question. Add the total you missed and subtract from 100. If you made a score of 70 or above, you are prepared to continue, having reviewed those items you missed. If you scored below 70, review those items you missed and go back in the text to review the topics pertaining to the missed items.

2. MATHEMATICAL PROOFS

MATHEMATICAL SYSTEMS

A mathematical system consists of the following:

a) a universal set
b) a set of relations
c) a set of operations
d) a set of axioms
e) a set of theorems
f) a set of definitions
g) rules of reasoning (logic)
h) undefined concepts

For example, in plane geometry the universal set was the set of points in the plane. The relations were such concepts as equality, perpendicularity, and parallelism. We previously considered the rules of reasoning. The undefined concepts were the points. Another example of a mathematical system is the system of real numbers; some axioms and properties of which are provided in the Appendix. We will often consider proofs in this system.

Every mathematical discourse is in reference to some mathematical system, even though it may not be clearly specified.

Definitions.

> "When I use a word," Humpty Dumpty said in a rather scornful tone, "it means just what I said it to mean - neither more nor less."
>
> Lewis Carroll, Through the Looking Glass.

A definition is an abbreviation. As abbreviations, definitions can be short, for example,

$$a < b \text{ iff } b > a$$

or long, for example,

f is integrable on $[a, b]$ iff $\displaystyle\lim_{\substack{x_j - x_{j-1} \to 0 \\ n \to \infty}} \sum_{j=1}^{n} f(\delta_j)(x_j - x_{j-1}) < \infty$.

You can always substitute an expression being defined for that which defines it, and conversely.

You should learn to read into a definition its "iff", or "equivalence" meaning. Definitions are often stated in a manner which conceals the possibility of substituting one expression for another due to an intended but not stated equivalence. For example, consider the definitions:

An even integer a is of the form a = 2k , k an integer
An integer a is even if a = 2k, k an integer.

Each could be restated:

An integer a is even iff a = 2k, k an integer.

Then, by the Rule of Substitution, either expression could be substituted for the other.

EXERCISES

Restate the definitions in 1 through 8 in "iff" form.

1. If a = 2k + 1, then a is odd.
2. A quadrilateral is a polygon with just four sides.
3. The maximum value of f on S, denoted $\max_S f$, is the largest value assumed by f on S.
4. A series is divergent if it is not convergent.
5. A triangle is a polygon with just four sides.
6. A real number is a number x that is equal to an infinite decimal.
7. A real number x which is not a rational number is an irrational number.
8. The complex numbers are the numbers of the form x + yi, where x and y are real numbers and $i^2 = -1$.
9. Find three examples of incorrectly stated definitions in mathematics textbooks.
10. Find a textbook where the student has first been taught the meaning of "iff" and in which most definitions are stated as equivalences.
11. Look up the definition of triangle congruence in a geometry text. Would you call this a long or short definition?

ANSWERS:

1. a = 2k + 1 iff a is odd.
2. A polygon is a quadrilateral iff it has just four sides.
3. $\max_S f$ is the maximum value of f on S iff it is the largest value assumed by f on S.
6. x is a real number iff x equals an infinite decimal.
7. x is irrational iff x is a real number which is not rational.
8. A number is complex iff it is of the form x + yi, where x and y are real numbers.
11. Long.

. . . .

Proof. Suppose $S_1, \ldots, S_n$ are all of the axioms and previously proved theorems in a mathematical system. A proof, or deduction, of a sentence P is a valid argument.

$$S_1, \ldots, S_n \vdash P$$

using the rules of reasoning.

A theorem is any sentence deduced from the axioms and/or the previously proved theorems.

EXERCISES

Suppose a certain mathematical system contained just the following axioms:

A_1 : $a + b = e \rightarrow [\, a + b = e \rightarrow (d + g = j \wedge g{*}p)\,]$
A_2 : $a + b = e$

Find all theorems deducible from the axioms.

ANSWERS:

A_1 : $a + b = e \rightarrow [\, a + b = e \rightarrow (d + g = j \wedge g{*}p)\,]$
A_2 : $a + b = e$

∴ Theorem 1: $a + b = e \rightarrow (d + g = j \wedge g{*}p)$, by modus ponens

$a + b = e \rightarrow (d + g = j \wedge g{*}p)$
$a + b = e$

∴ Theorem 2: $d + g = j \wedge g{*}p$, by modus ponens

$d + g = j \wedge g{*}p$
$(d + g = j \wedge g{*}p) \rightarrow d + g = j$: Tautology $(P \wedge Q) \rightarrow P$

∴ Theorem 3: $d + g = j$, modus ponens

$d + g = j \wedge g{*}p$
$(d + g = j \wedge g{*}p) \rightarrow g{*}p$: Tautology $(P \wedge Q) \rightarrow Q$

∴ Theorem 4: $g{*}p$

....

Developing a proof is considered to be an art. The art of mathematics is creating proofs. Just as a painter has some basic modes of painting, the mathematician has some basic modes of proof which we now consider.

PROVING SENTENCES OF THE TYPE $P \rightarrow Q$

Now we consider two modes of proof for sentences of the type $P \rightarrow Q$; later we consider others.

Rule of Conditional Proof - RCP. You usually proved a sentence of the type $P \rightarrow Q$ in plane geometry by assuming P and deducing Q. You considered Q the conclusion. In actuality

$$P \rightarrow Q$$

was the conclusion; it was what you were trying to prove.

To prove $P \rightarrow Q$ first assume P to be true (make it an axiom temporarily). Then using P and all other theorems and axioms try to deduce

Q. Once Q is deduced in this manner you have completed a proof of P → Q. You have not shown that Q is true; you have only shown that Q is true if P is true. Whether P is true is another question; whether Q is true is also another question. What you have shown to be true is P → Q.

To explain this more formally suppose $S_1, \ldots, S_n$ are the axioms and previously proved theorems. To prove P → Q is to show that

$$S_1, \ldots, S_n \vdash P \to Q$$

is a valid argument. To do this temporarily assume P is an axiom and show that

$$S_1, \ldots, S_n, P \vdash Q$$

is a valid argument. The above is referred to as <u>The Deduction Theorem</u>, though we consider it a proof axiom.

EXAMPLE. Recall: a is an integer iff a can be expressed in the form a = 2k, where k is some integer.

<u>Prove:</u> a is an even integer → a^2 is an even integer.

<u>Proof:</u> Assume a is an integer. Then a = 2k for some integer k. Hence $a^2 = 2(2k^2)$ and $2k^2$ is an integer, so a^2 is even. ● (Henceforth, ● will denote the completion of a proof.)

Within the previous proof we used the tautology

$$[(P \to S_1) \wedge (S_1 \to S_2) \wedge \ldots \wedge (S_n \to R)] \to (P \to R).$$

That is,

$$\text{a even} \to a = 2k \to a^2 = 2(2k^2) \to a^2 \text{ is even;}$$
$$\therefore \text{a even} \to a^2 \text{ is even.}$$

All proofs will be given in a paragraph style because this is the way experienced mathematicians write proofs. This style differs from the more difficult to write parallel column format used in plane geometry.

The <u>Rule of Conditional Proof</u> actually provides another (assumed) way to establish that a conditional sentence is true. To explain this note that the sentence

If grass is red, then 3 = 4 (1)

is true because the antecedent is false. This might be called "structural truth". Compare this with the sentence

If 4x + 5 = 13, then x = 2 (2)

Now any replacement for x which makes the antecedent 4x + 5 = 13 false, makes the sentence (2) true. So the only concern is whether (2) is true when 4x + 5 = 13 is true. To establish that (2) is true one establishes the truth of x = 2 based on the truth of 4x + 5 = 13. This might be called "truth by <u>dependence</u> of the consequent on the antecedent".

As an additional example of the <u>Rule of Conditional Proof</u> (RCP) we deduce another reasoning sentence.

<u>Theorem.</u> Every sentence of the type

$$\forall x P(x) \rightarrow \exists x P(x)$$

is true.

Proof. Assume $\forall x P(x)$ is true. Then the solution set for $P(x)$ is the universal set. Since universal sets are assumed to be non-empty the sentence $\exists x P(x)$ is true. ●

EXERCISE

Explain why $\forall x P(x) \rightarrow \exists x P(x)$ is true when $\forall x P(x)$ is false.

ANSWER:

The sentence is true by the truth table for '$\rightarrow$'.

....

Contrapositive. We can prove

$$P \rightarrow Q$$

by proving its contrapositive

$$\sim Q \rightarrow \sim P.$$

The two are equivalent.

EXAMPLE. The following proof is from Euclidean geometry. We assume the student has a knowledge of its axioms and properties.

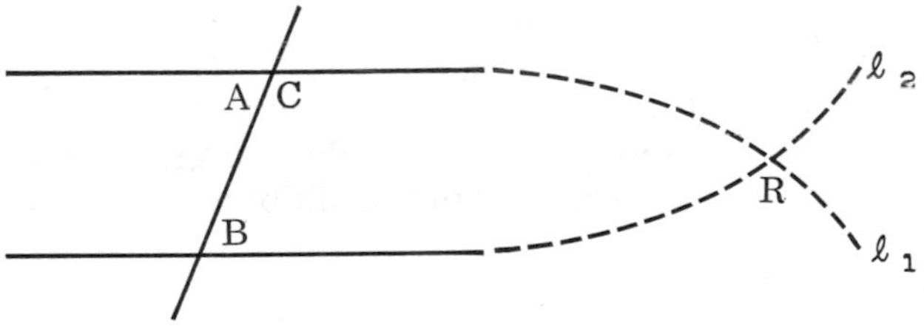

Prove: $\angle A = \angle B \rightarrow \ell_1 \cap \ell_2 = \emptyset$.

Proof. By contrapositive we will prove

$$\ell_1 \cap \ell_2 \neq \emptyset \rightarrow \angle A \neq \angle B$$

Assume $\ell_1 \cap \ell_2 \neq \emptyset$; that is, they intersect at a point R. Then RCB is a triangle, so $\angle C + \angle B + \angle R = 180°$. Also $\angle A$ and $\angle C$ are supplementary. Hence $\angle C + \angle B + \angle R = \angle A + \angle C$, so $\angle B + \angle R = \angle A$. Recall that the measure of any angle of a triangle is positive so $\angle R > 0$. Then $\angle B < \angle A$ (see P1 of the Appendix) or $\angle A \neq \angle B$. ●

Notice that in the previous proof the rule of conditional proof was used to prove the contrapositive.

EXERCISES

Consider

a^2 is an even integer → a is an even integer

1. State the contrapositive.
2. Prove the contrapositive.

ANSWERS:

1. a is an odd integer → a^2 is an odd integer.
2. Proof. Assume a is an odd integer. Then $a = 2k + 1$ for some integer k, so $a^2 = 4k^2 + 4k + 1 = 2(2k^2 + 2k) + 1$. Hence a^2 is an odd integer.

....

In summary, we have considered two ways of proving P → Q.

1) RCP. Assume P, deduce Q.
2) Contrapositive. Prove ~Q → ~ P; assume ~ Q and deduce ~ P.

Later we consider others.

EXERCISES

Give a direct proof of each of the following using RCP.

1. If a is even b is even, then a + b is even.
2. If a is even and b is even, then ab is even.
3. If a is even and b is odd, then a + b is odd.
4. If a is even and b is odd, then ab is even.
5. If a is odd and b is odd, then a + b is even.
6. If a is odd and b is odd, then ab is odd.
7. If a is odd, then a^2 is odd. (Although you are asked to give a proof here, do you see why it is unnecessary on the basis of what we have already proved?)
8. Prove: Every sentence of the type

   $\exists y \forall x P(x, y) \rightarrow \forall x \exists y P(x, y)$

   is true.

Give a proof by contrapositive of the sentences in Exercises 9 through 11.

9. If a^2 is odd, then a is odd. [Again, though you are asked to give the proof, do you see why it is unnecessary?]
10. A perfect number is a number which is the sum of its proper divisors. For example, 6 is a perfect number.

    Prove: If n is perfect, then n is not prime.
11. $[\forall \epsilon > 0 \ (|a| < \epsilon)] \rightarrow a = 0$.
12. Mathematicians often prove a sentence of the type $P \rightarrow (Q \wedge R)$ by proving P → Q and P → R. Find a tautology which justifies this.

13. Mathematicians often prove a sentence of the type $P \to (Q \to R)$ by proving $(P \wedge Q) \to R$. Find a tautology which justifies this.
14. Mathematicians often prove a sentence of the type $(P \to Q) \to (S \to R)$ by proving $[(P \to Q) \wedge S] \to R$. Justify this with a tautology.

ANSWERS:

2. Assume a even and b even. Then there exists integers k and m such that $a = 2k$ and $b = 2m$. Then $ab = (2k) \cdot (2m) = 2(k2m)$, so ab is even.
4. Assume a even and b odd. Then there exists integers k and m such that $a = 2k$ and $b = 2m + 1$. Then $ab = 2k(2m + 1)$, so ab is even.
8. Assume $\exists y \forall x P(x, y)$. There is a replacement b for y such that

   $\forall x\, P(x, b)$ is true.

   Thus for every u in the universal set

   $P(u, b)$ is true.

   Then b yields a true sentence for every u, so

   $\exists y(u, y)$ is true for every u.

   Hence,

   $\forall x \exists y\, (x, y)$ is true.

11. The contrapositive is

    $a \neq 0 \to \exists \epsilon > 0(|a| \geq \epsilon)$.

    Now

    $a \neq 0 \to |a| > 0$

    by P2 of the appendix. So there exists an $\epsilon > 0$ such that $|a| \geq \epsilon$, namely $\epsilon = |a|$.
12. $[P \to (Q \wedge R)] \leftrightarrow [(P \to Q) \wedge (P \to R)]$
13. $[(P \to Q) \to (S \to R)] \leftrightarrow [((P \to Q) \wedge S) \to R]$

....

PROVING SENTENCES OF THE TYPE $P \leftrightarrow Q$

We consider three modes of proof for sentences of the type $P \leftrightarrow Q$.

Prove $P \to Q$ and $Q \to P$. One mode of proof for

$P \leftrightarrow Q$

is derived from its definition.

EXERCISE

Complete.

$P \leftrightarrow Q$ iff ____________

ANSWER:

$(P \to Q) \wedge (Q \to P)$

••

Thus there are two steps in the proof

a) Prove $P \to Q$; referred to as the "if part", or the "sufficiency" part.

b) Prove $Q \to P$; referred to us the "only if" part or the "necessity" part.

Each of these sentences is a conditional which might be proved using previously considered modes of proof.

EXAMPLE. Prove: Real numbers a and b are roots of the equation $x^2 + px + q = 0$ iff $a + b = -p$ and $ab = q$.

Proof: a) (If or sufficiency part)

Prove: if a and b are roots of $x^2 + px + q = 0$, then $a + b = p$ and $ab = q$.

Using RCP, assume a and b are roots of the equation. Then via the quadratic formula we know that

$$a = \frac{-p + \sqrt{p^2 - 4q}}{2} \quad \text{and} \quad b = \frac{-p - \sqrt{p^2 - 4q}}{2}$$

[The signs +, - could be interchanged without affecting the proof.]

Then $a + b = -p$ and $ab = q$, by algebra.

b) (Only if or necessity part)

Prove: if $a + b = -p$ and $ab = q$, then a and b are roots of the equation $x^2 + px + q = 0$.

Again using RCP assume $a + b = -p$ and $ab = q$. Then $a + b = -p$ implies $b = -p - a$ so $(-p - a)a = -pa - a^2 = q$. Hence $a^2 + pa + q = 0$, so a is a root of $x^2 + px + q = 0$. ●

Prove $P \to Q$ and $\sim P \to \sim Q$. Another mode of proof for

$$P \leftrightarrow Q$$

is to prove

$$P \to Q,$$

as before, but then prove the contrapositive of $Q \to P$,

$$\sim P \to \sim Q$$

EXAMPLE. Prove: a is even iff a^2 is even

EXERCISE

To use the mode of proof just described list the sentences to be proved.

1. ______________________ 2. ______________________

ANSWERS:

1. a even $\rightarrow$ a^2 even
2. a not even (odd) $\rightarrow$ a^2 not even (odd)

....

We have given these proofs in previous examples.

Iff-string. A third mode of proof for

$$P \leftrightarrow Q$$

is accomplished by producing a string of equivalent sentences leading from P to Q as follows.

$$\begin{array}{lll} P \leftrightarrow Q_1 & & P \leftrightarrow Q_1 \\ Q_1 \leftrightarrow Q_2 & \text{abbreviated} & \quad\leftrightarrow Q_2 \\ \vdots & & \quad\vdots \\ Q_n \leftrightarrow Q & & \quad\leftrightarrow Q \end{array}$$

Once each of the previous is proved $P \leftrightarrow Q$ follows by a tautology.

EXERCISE

What tautology justifies the above? ______________________

ANSWER:

$[(P \leftrightarrow Q_1) \wedge \ldots \wedge (Q_n \leftrightarrow Q)] \rightarrow (P \leftrightarrow Q)$

....

EXAMPLE. Prove. Every sentence of the type

$$\forall x \forall y\, P(x, y) \leftrightarrow \forall y \forall x\, P(x, y)$$

is true.

Proof. Using Iff-string we have

$\forall x \forall y\, P(x, y)$ is true $\leftrightarrow$ for every replacement of x and y by members a and b of the universal set P(a, b) is true.

$\leftrightarrow$ for every replacement of y and x by members a and b of the universal set P(a, b) is true.

$\leftrightarrow$ $\forall y \forall x\, P(x, y)$ is true. ●

Many more examples of this mode of proof will be given in the section on set theory.

In summary, we have considered three modes of proof for sentences of the type $P \leftrightarrow Q$:

a) <u>Prove $P \rightarrow Q$ and $Q \rightarrow P$.</u> ($Q \rightarrow P$ is called the <u>converse</u> of $P \rightarrow Q$)
b) <u>Prove $P \rightarrow Q$ and $\sim P \rightarrow \sim Q$.</u> ($\sim P \rightarrow \sim Q$ is called the <u>inverse</u> of $P \rightarrow Q$)
c) <u>Iff-string.</u> Produce a string of equivalent sentences leading from P to Q.

EXERCISES

Prove the sentences in Exercises 1 through 7.

1. a is an odd integer $\leftrightarrow a^2$ is an odd integer.
2. Consider the figure

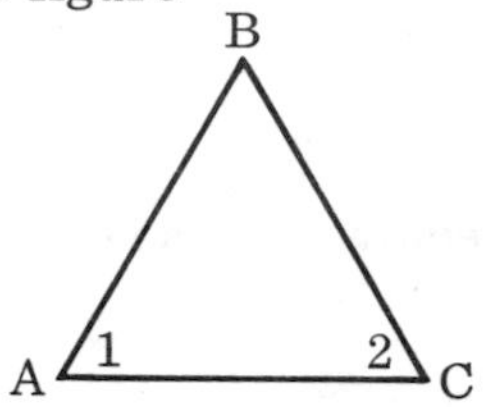

Prove: $AB = BC \leftrightarrow \angle 1 = \angle 2$

Use congruence properties of geometry.

3. $a < b \leftrightarrow a + c < b + c$. Use the real number properties of the Appendix.
4. x is an odd integer iff $x + 1$ is an even integer.
5. x is an even integer iff $x + 2$ is an even integer.
6. Every sentence of the type

$$\exists x \exists y\, P(x, y) \leftrightarrow \exists y \exists x\, P(x, y)$$

is true.

7. Every sentence of the type

$$\forall x [P(x) \wedge Q(x)] \leftrightarrow [\forall x P(x) \wedge \forall x Q(x)]$$

is true.

8. Mathematicians often prove a sentence of the type $P \rightarrow (Q \leftrightarrow R)$ by proving $(P \wedge Q) \rightarrow R$ and $(P \wedge R) \rightarrow Q$. Find a tautology which justifies this.

ANSWERS:

1. Prove:

a odd $\rightarrow a^2$ odd

and

a not odd (even) $\rightarrow a^2$ not odd (even)

Both proofs have been given before.

3. a) Prove: $a < b \rightarrow a + c < b + c$. This holds by 03 of the Appendix.
b) Prove: $a + c < b + c \rightarrow a < b$. Assume $a + c < b + c$. Then by A4 and 03,

$$(a + c) + (^-c) < (b + c) + {}^-c$$

and by A2, A3, and A4

$$a + [c + (^{-}c)] < b + [c + (^{-}c)]$$
$$a + 0 < b + 0$$
$$a < b$$

4. a) Prove: x odd → x + 1 even
   Assume x odd. Then for some integer k, $x = 2 \cdot k + 1$. Then

$$x + 1 = 2k + 2$$
$$= 2(k + 1)$$

so x + 1 is even.

b) Prove: x + 1 even → x odd
   Assume x + 1 even. Then for some k

$$x + 1 = 2 \cdot k$$
$$x = 2 \cdot k - 1$$
$$= 2k - 1 + 2 - 2$$
$$= 2k - 2 + 1$$
$$= 2(k - 1) + 1$$

so x is odd.

8. $[P \rightarrow (Q \leftrightarrow R)] \leftrightarrow [(P \wedge Q) \rightarrow R \wedge (P \wedge R) \rightarrow Q]$

....

PROVING SENTENCES OF THE TYPE ∀x P(x)

To prove

$\forall x\, P(x)$,

let x represent an arbitrary element of the universal set and prove

$P(x)$

true. Then since x was an arbitrary element of the universal set generalize

$\forall x\, P(x)$

true.

EXAMPLE. Consider

∀ *f* (*f* is differentiable → *f* is continuous.

To prove the sentence let *f* be an arbitrary function and prove

"*f* differentiable → *f* is continuous."

By RCP, assume *f* differentiable and prove *f* continuous. We will not include the proof; it appears in most calculus texts. Once we have proved

"*f* differentiable → *f* is continuous"

we have proved

"∀ *f* (*f* is differentiable → *f* is continuous)",

since f was an arbitrary function.

EXAMPLES. a) Consider

$$\forall x(1 < x \rightarrow 1 < x^2)$$

with universal set $\{2, 3\}$. Considering

$$1 < 2 \rightarrow 1 < 2^2$$

and

$$1 < 3 \rightarrow 1 < 3^2,$$

we have proved the sentence by substitution.

b) Consider

$$\forall x(1 < x \rightarrow 1 < x^2)$$

with infinite universal set N. Trying to prove the sentence by substituting each element would be impossible. To do the proof let x be arbitrary and prove

$$1 < x \rightarrow 1 < x^2.$$

Such a proof would depend on the axioms for N (See Appendix) which are stated in terms of quantifiers.

Proof. Assume $1 < x$. Then since $1 > 0$, by 06, it follows that $x > 0$ by 02. Then $1 < x$ and $x > 0$ implies $1 \cdot x < x \cdot x$, by O4. So $1 < x$ and $x < x^2$ implies $1 < x^2$, by O2. Therefore,

$$1 < x \rightarrow 1 < x^2,$$

so

$$\forall x(1 < x \rightarrow 1 < x^2)$$

is proved.●

PROVING SENTENCES OF THE TYPE $\exists x\, P(x)$

To prove $\exists x\, P(x)$ show or prove there exists an x in the universal set for which P(x) is true.

EXAMPLE.

Prove: $\exists f$ (f is continuous $\wedge$ f is not differentiable)
Proof. The function described by $f(x) = |x|$ is continuous but not differentiable.●

We will comment about another mode of proof for $\exists x\, P(x)$ when we consider proof by contradiction.

EXERCISES

Describe the modes of proof you might use to prove each of the following.

1. $\forall x$(x^3 is even iff x is even).

2. $\forall a \forall b(a < b \text{ iff } a + 8 < b + 8)$.
3. For any two sets A, and B, $x \in A \cup B$ iff $x \in B \cup A$.
4. For any set A, $A \subset A$.
5. For any set A, $\emptyset \subset A$.
6. $\exists x(x^2 = x)$
7. $\exists \{u_n\} (\sum_{n=1}^{\infty} u_n \text{ is divergent} \wedge \lim_{n \to \infty} u_n = 0)$
8. $\exists y \forall x(x + y = x)$
9. $\exists y \forall x(xy = x)$

ANSWERS:

1. Let x be arbitrary. Prove

   "x^2 is even iff x is even"

   by proving
   a) If x^2 is even, then x is even.
   b) If x is even, then x^2 is even.
8. Show or prove there exists a y such that $\forall x(x + y = x)$. To do this let x be arbitrary and prove $x + y = x$.

....

MORE ON PROOFS

A typical comment made when proofs are attempted is "I do not know where to start". While there is no royal road to success there are some helpful procedures to follow.

Translate to Logical Symbolism. Translate the sentence to be proved to logical symbolism. Examine the translated sentence and think of a mode, or modes of proof which could be used to prove it.

To illustrate, suppose you are to prove a sentence of the type

P is a sufficient condition for Q.

Translating to logical symbolism we have

$$P \rightarrow Q.$$

Thus far we have considered two modes of proof for this sentence:

a) RCP. Assume P, deduce Q.
b) Contrapositive. Assume $\sim Q$, deduce $\sim P$.

It is hoped that you would think of these

Another comment that arises when attempting to use a mode of proof, say RCP, is "I want to assume P and deduce Q, but how do I get from P to Q?" There is again no royal road to success; certainly knowing to assume P and deduce Q is a step in the right direction. The mode of proof provides the structure for the proof; building this structure is usually a more creative task. The following are a few procedures helpful in carrying out modes of proof.

Analogy. In a previous example we gave the proof of

$$a \text{ is even} \rightarrow a^2 \text{ is even.}$$

In the exercises which followed you proved

$$a \text{ is odd} \rightarrow a^2 \text{ is odd.}$$

Did you notice that the proofs were analogous? That is, the proof in the example should have suggested a way of proving the sentence in the exercise.

Thus an important aid in carrying out proofs is to get ideas from other proofs. This is supported by comments of mathematicians who argue that to be good at mathematics you need lots of practice; lots of exposure to different proofs.

Analytic Process. (Working backwards) You want to prove $P \rightarrow Q$. Start with Q and try to find an R such that $R \rightarrow Q$. Then try to find a S such that $S \rightarrow R$. Then you might discover that $P \rightarrow S$.

Assume: P
Deduce: Q
Analytic Process: Q if R ($R \rightarrow Q$) Hence $P \rightarrow S \rightarrow R \rightarrow Q$
R if S ($S \rightarrow R$) $\therefore$ $P \rightarrow Q$
S if P ($P \rightarrow S$)

When reading a proof of $P \rightarrow Q$ in a text one may only see the sequence $P \rightarrow S \rightarrow R \rightarrow Q$ and be amazed at how the author came about it. If the analytic process was used, it probably was not mentioned.

EXAMPLE. Consider $\triangle ABC$.

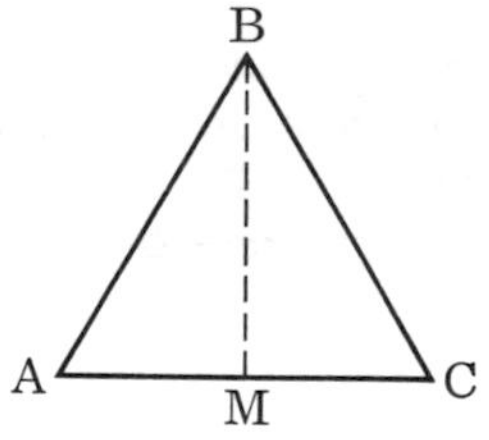

Prove: $\overline{AB} \cong \overline{CB} \rightarrow \angle A = \angle C$.

Proof: Assume: $\overline{AB} \cong \overline{CB}$

Deduce: $\angle A = \angle B$

Consider $\angle A$ and $\angle C$. These angles would be congruent if they were corresponding angles of congruent triangles. You might think of drawing a segment from B to the midpoint M, of $\overline{AC}$. Then analytically,

$\angle A = \angle C$ if $\triangle AMB \cong \triangle CMB$ (SSS)

$\triangle AMB \cong \triangle CMB$ if a) $\overline{BM} \cong \overline{BM}$ (Same segment)

b) $\overline{AM} \cong \overline{CM}$ ($\overline{BM}$ bisects $\overline{AC}$)

c) $\overline{AB} \cong \overline{CB}$ (Assumed)

Then the proof would begin with steps (c), (b), and (a); deduce $\triangle AMB \cong \triangle CMB$ and $\angle A \cong \angle C$. ●

Starting with the Conclusion. Care should be taken to note that the use of the Analytic Process is logically valid. The process we are about to describe may not be logically valid, but could lead to a valid argument (a proof).

Suppose you want to prove $P \rightarrow Q$, start with Q and deduce as much as you can from it. For example, you might have

$Q \rightarrow X \rightarrow S \rightarrow P.$

EXERCISE

Why is this not a proof? ________________________________

ANSWER:

$(Q \rightarrow P) \rightarrow (P \rightarrow Q)$ is not a tautology.

....

Though the previous was not a proof you could try to retrace the steps to see if the implications could be turned around:

$$\begin{array}{ccccccc} Q & \rightarrow & X & \rightarrow & S & \rightarrow & P \\ & \overset{\leftarrow}{?} & & \overset{\leftarrow}{?} & & \overset{\leftarrow}{?} & \end{array}$$

If so, then

$P \rightarrow S \rightarrow X \rightarrow Q$

$\therefore P \rightarrow Q$

and you have a proof.

EXAMPLE. Obtaining extraneous roots. To solve the equation

$5 + \sqrt{x+7} = x, \ (x \in R)$

we could assume x is a number such that $5 + \sqrt{x+7} = x$. Note that what we are looking for is the solution, but we start by assuming we already have it. Then

$$\begin{aligned} 5 + \sqrt{x+7} = x &\rightarrow \sqrt{x+7} = x - 5 \\ &\rightarrow x + 7 = (x-5)^2 \\ &\rightarrow x^2 - 11x + 18 = 0 \\ &\rightarrow (x-9)(x+2) = 0 \end{aligned}$$

$$\to x = 9 \lor x = 2$$

What we have shown is

$$5 + \sqrt{x + 7} = x \to x = 9 \lor x = 2.$$

We must determine the truth of

$$x = 9 \lor x = 2 \to 5 + \sqrt{x + 7} = x$$

Checking,

$$5 + \sqrt{9 + 7} = 5 + 4 = 9$$

$$5 + \sqrt{2 + 7} = 5 + 3 = 8 \neq 2$$

We see that,

if $x = 9$ then $5 + \sqrt{x + 7} = x$.

Invalid reasoning would have produced the extraneous root $x = 2$.

EXAMPLE. Given $f(x) = 2x + 1$ and $\epsilon > 0$. Find a $\delta > 0$ such that

$$|x| < \delta \to |f(x) - 1| < \epsilon .$$

Start with

$$|f(x) - 1| < \epsilon .$$

Then

$$\begin{aligned} |f(x) - 1| < \epsilon &\to |(2x + 1) - 1| < \epsilon \\ &\to |2x| < \epsilon \\ &\to -\epsilon < 2x < \epsilon \\ &\to -\epsilon/2 < x < \epsilon/2 \\ &\to |x| < \epsilon/2 \end{aligned}$$

Checking backwards we see that each arrow could be reversed; that is, for $\delta = \epsilon/2$,

$$|x| < \delta \to |f(x) - 1| < \epsilon . \qquad (1)$$

Often in such a proof an author will say "Let $\delta = \epsilon/2$" and then prove (1). What puzzles one is how he knew to let $\delta = \epsilon/2$. The author knew because he had started with the conclusion and proceeded as above.

Remember to watch your logic when you start with the conclusion!

Do-Something Approach. (Trial and error) You want to prove $P \to Q$ by assuming P and deducing Q. You have no particular way to get from P to Q; but start out, get involved, do something, try different approaches, prove all you can. You might happen onto the proof. This could be illustrated as follows:

$P \to R \to T \to S$	?,
$P \to M \to Y \to Z \to V$	?,
$P \to W \to X \to Q$	success!

The do-something approach can also be used with the modes of proof. You try RCP and get nowhere. Maybe, you can prove the contrapositive.

When reading proofs in mathematics texts and journals, one is not aware of the blind alleys and unsuccessful attempts preceding a successful proof. This leads one to think the established mathematician never follows a blind alley or makes a mistake. Trial and error is very much a part of mathematics.

Use of Definitions. Another helpful procedure is to recall all relevant definitions. It is a tendency to read a definition and ignore its importance in later proofs. To illustrate, suppose the following definition is given in set theory.

Definition. For any two sets A and B,

$$A \subset B \text{ iff for every } x,\ x \in A \rightarrow x \in B.$$

Later the following theorem is to be proved.

Theorem. For any two sets A and B.

$$A \cap B \subset A.$$

To accomplish the proof one would let A and B be arbitrary sets and prove $A \cap B \subset A$. A stumbling block may be met at this point unless one uses the definition to interpret what it means for $A \cap B$ to be contained in A. That is, using the definition it follows that one must prove,

$$\text{For every } x,\ x \in A \cap B \rightarrow x \in A.$$

Use of Previously Proved Theorems. It is also helpful in starting a proof to examine previously proved theorems for results which might be relevant to a proof you are attempting.

EXERCISES

1. Describe now the analytic process that could be used to prove the contrapositive of $P \rightarrow Q$.
2. Describe now the analytic process that could be used to prove $P \rightarrow \sim Q$.

   Assume the following are proved:
   a) $A \cup B = B \cup A$
   b) $(A \cup B) \cup C = A \cup (B \cup C)$
   c) $x \in Q \wedge y \in J \rightarrow x + y \in J$
   d) The solution of $5 + \sqrt{x + 7} = x$ is $x = 9$.
   e) $A \subset B \rightarrow \complement B \subset \complement A$
   f) $\int (f + g) = \int f + \int g$
   g) $A \cup (B \cap C) = (A \cup B) \cap (A \cup C)$
   h) $\complement (A \cup B) = \complement A \cap \complement B$

Suppose that you wanted to prove the sentences in Exercises 3 through 10. State an analogous proof for an above sentence you might examine for a hint.

3. $B \subset \complement A \rightarrow A \subset \complement B$

4. $\left| \int f + g \right| \leq \int | f | + \int | g |$
5. $A \cap B = B \cap A$
6. There is a solution for $\sqrt{2x - 1} = x - 2$
7. $x \in Q \wedge y \in J \rightarrow x - y \in J$
8. $(A \cap B) \cap C = A \cap (B \cap C)$
9. $A \cap (B \cup C) = (A \cap B) \cup (A \cap C)$
10. $\complement (A \cap B) = \complement A \cup \complement B$
11. Find the solution for Exercise 6.
12. Given $f(x) = 3x + 2$ and $\epsilon > 0$. Find a $\delta > 0$ such that

$$|x| < \delta \rightarrow |f(x) - 2| < \epsilon .$$

ANSWERS:

1. Assume: $\sim Q$
   Deduce: $\sim P$
   Analytic Process: $\sim P$ if $R(R \rightarrow \sim P)$
   R if $S(S \rightarrow R)$
   S if $\sim Q(\sim Q \rightarrow S)$

   Hence $\sim Q \rightarrow S \rightarrow R \rightarrow \sim P$
   $\therefore \sim Q \rightarrow \sim P$

3. e	4. f	5. a	6. d	7. c	8. b
9. g	10. h	11. $x = 5$	12. $\delta = \epsilon/3$		

....

APPLICATIONS TO SET THEORY

To illustrate the utility of the logic and modes of proof examined thus far we consider some proofs from set theory. In many proofs we mention the mode(s) of proof used. When a mode is not mentioned you should decide what is used. The analysis notes occuring at the end of many proofs explain how the proofs might have been conceived.

Let U be a universal set (a set of undefined objects). Recall that

$$a \in A$$

means

a is an element of A

(ϵ is an undefined relation between the objects of sets and sets themselves).

<u>Axiom 1.</u> (Equality) $A = B \leftrightarrow \forall x(x \in A \leftrightarrow x \in B)$

<u>Axiom 2.</u> $A = U \leftrightarrow \forall x(x \in A)$; $\forall x(x \in U)$

<u>Axiom 3.</u> $A = \emptyset \leftrightarrow \forall x(x \notin A)$; $\forall x(x \notin \emptyset)$

<u>Axiom 4.</u> $U \neq \emptyset$

<u>Axiom 5.</u> $A \notin A$; $x \neq \{x\}$

Axiom 6 (Specification) If for every $x \in U$, $P(x)$ is a statement, then there exists a set B such that

$$x \in B \leftrightarrow P(x);$$

that is,

$$B = \{ x \mid x \in U \wedge P(x) \}.$$

Definition 1. $A \subset B \leftrightarrow \forall x(x \in A \rightarrow x \in B)$;
that is, for every $x \in U$,

if $x \in A$, then $x \in B$.

Definition 2. $A \cup B = \{ x \mid x \in A \vee x \in B \}$;
that is,

$$x \in A \cup B \leftrightarrow x \in A \vee x \in B.$$

Definition 3. $A \cap B = \{ x \mid x \in A \wedge x \in B \}$;
that is,

$$x \in A \cap B \leftrightarrow x \in A \wedge x \in B.$$

Definition 4. $\complement A = \{ x \mid x \notin A \} = \{ x \mid x \in U \wedge x \notin A \}$,
or more conveniently

$$x \in \complement A \leftrightarrow x \notin A$$

since we agree to consider only subsets of U and hence only elements of subsets of U.

Definition 5. $\mathcal{P}(A) = \{ B \mid B \subset A \}$

Theorem 1. $A = \emptyset \leftrightarrow \sim \exists x(x \in A)$

Proof. $A = \emptyset \leftrightarrow \forall x(x \notin A)$, by Axiom 3
$\leftrightarrow \sim \exists x(x \in A)$, by a rule for negating quantified sentences. ●

ANALYSIS: Recollection of the rules for negating quantified sentences.

Theorem 2. $A = B \leftrightarrow A \subset B \wedge B \subset A$.

Proof. Mode of proof: Iff-string.

$A = B \leftrightarrow \forall x(x \in A \leftrightarrow x \in B)$, by Axiom 1
$\leftrightarrow \forall x[(x \in A \rightarrow x \in B) \wedge (x \in B \rightarrow x \in A)]$, by the definition of '$\leftrightarrow$' and the rule of substitution.
$\leftrightarrow \forall x(x \in A \rightarrow x \in B) \wedge \forall x(x \in B \rightarrow x \in A)$, by the rule of reasoning $\forall x[P(x) \wedge Q(x)] \leftrightarrow [\forall x P(x) \wedge \forall x Q(x)]$.
$\leftrightarrow A \subset B \wedge B \subset A$, by Definition 1. ●

ANALYSIS: Applying the definition of '$\leftrightarrow$'.

Theorem 2 provides a very useful way of proving two sets equal.

Theorem 3. For every subset A of U,

$$\emptyset \subset A.$$

Proof. We are proving the sentence $\forall A(\emptyset \subset A)$ where the quantifier refers to the set of all subsets of U, $\mathcal{P}(U)$. Let A represent an arbitrary subset of U. [Recall that this is one way to prove a sentence of the type

$\forall xP(x)$.] We must prove $\emptyset \subset A$. Now

$$\emptyset \subset A \leftrightarrow \forall x(x \in \emptyset \rightarrow x \in A).$$

But we know that $\forall x(x \notin \emptyset)$ by Axiom 3; that is,

for every $x \in U$, $x \notin \emptyset$.

Hence $x \in \emptyset$ is false for every x in U. Since the conditional

$$x \in \emptyset \rightarrow x \in A$$

always has a <u>false</u> antecedent it is always true. Hence

$$\forall x(x \in \emptyset \rightarrow x \in A)$$

is true. We know

$$\emptyset \subset A \leftrightarrow \forall x(x \in \emptyset \rightarrow x \in A)$$

and we have proved

$$\forall x(x \in \emptyset \rightarrow x \in A).$$

Hence

$$\emptyset \subset A$$

by the rule of substitution. Since we have proved this for an arbitrary A we have proved

$$\forall A(\emptyset \subset A). \bullet$$

<u>Theorem 4.</u> For any two subsets A and B of U,

$$A \cap B = B \cap A.$$

<u>Proof.</u> We are proving the sentence $\forall A \forall B(A \cap B = B \cap A)$. Let A and B be arbitrary subsets of U. To prove

$$A \cap B = B \cap A$$

prove, using Axiom 1,

$$\forall x(x \in A \cap B \leftrightarrow x \in B \cap A).$$

Let x be an arbitrary element of U. Now

$$\begin{aligned} x \in A \cap B &\leftrightarrow (x \in A \wedge x \in B), \text{ by Definition 3} \\ &\leftrightarrow (x \in B \wedge x \in A), \text{ by the tautology } P \wedge Q \leftrightarrow Q \wedge P \\ &\leftrightarrow (x \in B \cap A), \text{ by Definition 3.} \end{aligned}$$

Hence $(x \in A \cap B) \leftrightarrow (x \in B \cap A)$, by <u>Iff-string.</u> Thus

$$\forall x(x \in A \cap B \leftrightarrow x \in B \cap A)$$

since x was an arbitrary element of U. Hence $A \cap B = B \cap A$ by Axiom 1, so $\forall A \forall B(A \cap B = B \cap A). \bullet$

ANALYSIS: The analogy between $A \cap B = B \cap A$ and the tautology $P \wedge Q \leftrightarrow Q \wedge P$ provided the idea for the proof.

<u>Theorem 5.</u> For any subset A of U,

$$C\,C\,A = A.$$

Proof. Let A be an arbitrary subset of U. Prove

$$\forall x(x \in \complement\complement A \leftrightarrow x \in A).$$

Let x be an arbitrary element of U. Now

$x \in \complement\complement A \leftrightarrow x \notin \complement A$, by Definition 4
$\leftrightarrow \sim (x \in \complement A)$, by definition of the negation symbol
$\leftrightarrow \sim (x \notin A)$, by Definition 4
$\leftrightarrow \sim\sim (x \in A)$, by definition of the negation symbol
$\leftrightarrow x \in A$, by the tautology $\sim\sim P \leftrightarrow P$.

Hence

$$\forall x(x \in \complement\complement A \leftrightarrow x \in A)$$

and it follows that

$$\complement\complement A = A$$

for every subset A of U. ●
ANALYSIS: Note the analogy between $\complement\complement A = A$ and $\sim\sim P \leftrightarrow P$.

Theorem 6. For any two subsets A and B of U,

$$A \subset B \leftrightarrow A \cap \complement B = \emptyset.$$

Proof. Let A and B be arbitrary subsets of U. Using Iff-string

$A \subset B \leftrightarrow \forall x(x \in A \rightarrow x \in B)$, by Definition 1
$\leftrightarrow \sim \exists x \sim(x \in A \rightarrow x \in B)$, by a rule for negating quantified sentences.
$\leftrightarrow \sim \exists x(x \in A \wedge x \notin B)$, by the tautology $\sim (P \rightarrow Q) \leftrightarrow (P \wedge \sim Q)$
$\leftrightarrow \sim \exists x(x \in A \wedge x \in \complement B)$, by Definition 4
$\leftrightarrow \sim \exists x(x \in A \cap \complement B)$, by Definition 3
$\leftrightarrow A \cap \complement B = \emptyset$, by Theorem 1

Hence $A \subset B \leftrightarrow A \cap \complement B = \emptyset$, for any two subsets A and B of U. ●
ANALYSIS: This proof was conceived by the author by starting with the definition of $A \subset B$ and deriving everything he could until the conditions of Theorem 1 were satisfied.

Theorem 7. For any two subsets A and B of U,

$$\complement(A \cup B) = \complement A \cap \complement B.$$

Proof. Let A and B be arbitrary subsets of U. We must show that

$$\forall x[x \in \complement(A \cup B) \leftrightarrow x \in \complement A \cap \complement B].$$

Let x be an arbitrary element of U. Using Iff-string

$x \in \complement(A \cup B) \leftrightarrow x \notin A \cup B$, by Definition 4
$\leftrightarrow \sim (x \in A \cup B)$, by definition of the negation symbol
$\leftrightarrow \sim (x \in A \vee x \in B)$, by Definition 2
$\leftrightarrow x \notin A \wedge x \notin B$, by the tautology $(\sim P \wedge \sim Q) \leftrightarrow \sim (P \vee Q)$
$\leftrightarrow x \in \complement A \wedge x \in \complement B$, by Definition 4
$\leftrightarrow x \in \complement A \cap \complement B$, by Definition 3

Hence

$$\forall x(x \in \complement(A \cup B) \leftrightarrow x \in \complement A \cap \complement B).$$

Therefore, for any two subsets A and B of U, $\complement(A \cup B) = \complement A \cap \complement B$. ●

The following theorem makes use of Theorems 5 and 7.

Theorem 8. For any two sets A and B,

$$\complement(A \cap B) = \complement A \cup \complement B.$$

Proof. Let A and B be arbitrary subsets of U. Now

$$\begin{aligned}\complement[\complement A \cup \complement B] &= \complement\complement A \cap \complement\complement B, \text{ by Theorem 7}\\ &= A \cap B, \text{ by Theorem 5}\end{aligned}$$

If $\complement[\complement A \cup \complement B] = A \cap B$, then

$$\complement\complement[\complement A \cup \complement B] = \complement(A \cap B).$$

[We will prove in the Exercises that $A = B \leftrightarrow \complement A = \complement B$]. By Theorem 5,

$$\complement\complement[\complement A \cup \complement B] = \complement A \cup \complement B,$$

Hence for every two subsets A and B of U,

$$\complement(A \cap B) = \complement A \cup \complement B. \bullet$$

Theorem 9. For any subsets A, B, and C, of U,

$$A \cap (B \cup C) = (A \cap B) \cup (A \cap C).$$

Proof. Let A, B, and C be arbitrary subsets of U. Prove

$$\forall x[x \in A \cap (B \cup C) \leftrightarrow x \in (A \cap B) \cup (A \cap C)].$$

Let x be an arbitrary element of U. Then

$$\begin{aligned}x \in A \cap (B \cup C) &\leftrightarrow x \in A \wedge x \in (B \cup C), \text{ by Definition 3}\\ &\leftrightarrow x \in A \wedge (x \in B \vee x \in C), \text{ by Definition 2}\\ &\leftrightarrow (x \in A \wedge x \in B) \vee (x \in A \wedge x \in C), \text{ by the tautology}\\ &\qquad P \wedge (Q \vee R) \leftrightarrow (P \wedge Q) \vee (P \wedge R)\\ &\leftrightarrow x \in (A \cap B) \cup (A \cap C), \text{ by Definition 2 and 3}\end{aligned}$$

Hence

$$\forall x[x \in A \cap (B \cup C) \leftrightarrow x \in (A \cap B) \cup (A \cap C)].$$

Hence for any subsets A, B, and C of U,

$$A \cap (B \cup C) = (A \cap B) \cup (A \cap C). \bullet$$

ANALYSIS: Note the similarity between $A \cap (B \cup C) = (A \cap B) \cup (A \cap C)$ and the tautology $P \wedge (Q \vee R) \leftrightarrow (P \wedge Q) \vee (P \wedge R)$.

Theorem 10. For any two subsets A and B of U,

$$A \subset A \cup B.$$

Proof. Let A and B be arbitrary subsets of U. Prove

$$A \subset A \cup B.$$

Now by definition,

$$A \subset A \cup B \leftrightarrow \forall x(x \in A \rightarrow x \in A \cup B).$$

Let x be an arbitrary element of U.

$$\begin{aligned} x \in A &\rightarrow x \in A \vee x \in B, \text{ by the tautology } P \rightarrow (P \vee Q) \\ &\rightarrow x \in (A \cup B), \text{ by Definition 2} \end{aligned}$$

Hence

$$x \in A \rightarrow x \in (A \cup B).$$

So for every x in U, $x \in A \rightarrow x \in (A \cup B)$. Hence

$$\forall A \forall B(A \subset A \cup B). \bullet$$

ANALYSIS: Note the similarity between $A \subset (A \cup B)$ and the tautology $P \rightarrow (P \vee Q)$.

Theorem 11. For any two subsets A and B of U,

$$A \subset B \rightarrow \complement B \subset \complement A$$

Proof. Let A and B be arbitrary subsets of U. Prove

$$A \subset B \rightarrow \complement B \subset \complement A.$$

Now

$$\begin{aligned} A \subset B &\rightarrow \forall x(x \in A \rightarrow x \in B), \text{ by Definition 1} \\ &\rightarrow \forall x(x \notin B \rightarrow x \notin A), \text{ using the contrapositive of } x \in A \rightarrow x \in B. \\ &\rightarrow \forall x(x \in \complement B \rightarrow x \in \complement A), \text{ by Definition 4} \\ &\rightarrow \complement B \subset \complement A, \text{ by Definition 1} \end{aligned}$$

Hence $A \subset B \rightarrow \complement B \subset \complement A$ for every two subsets A and B of U. $\bullet$

ANALYSIS: Note the similarity between $A \subset B \rightarrow \complement B \subset \complement A$ and the tautology $(P \rightarrow Q) \rightarrow (\sim Q \rightarrow \sim P)$.

EXERCISES

When doing these proofs note what mode(s) of proof you are using. Also, include your own analysis notes; that is, what provided the bud of the idea for the proof. For example, did you use a proof analogous to a previous one, did you use the do-something approach, and so on. Use any previous theorem or exercise for doing a proof. Compare your proof with that of the answer; they may differ.

Let A, B, and C be arbitrary subsets of U. Prove the following.

1. $A \subset A$
2. $A \cup B = B \cup A$
3. $A \subset B$ iff $\complement A \cup B = U$
4. $A \cap B \subset A$
5. $A \cup (B \cap C) = (A \cup B) \cap (A \cup C)$
6. $A \cup (B \cup C) = (A \cup B) \cup C$
7. $A \cap (B \cap C) = (A \cap B) \cap C$
8. $A \cup \emptyset = A$ Hint: Use Theorem 2 and 9.
9. $A \cup \complement A = U$ Hint: $P \vee \sim P$ is a tautology.

10. $\complement \emptyset = U$
11. $A = B \leftrightarrow \complement A = \complement B$
12. $\emptyset = \complement U$
13. $A \cap \emptyset = \emptyset$ Hint: Theorems 2, 3 and Exercise 4.
14. $A \subset U$
15. $A \cap U = A$; $A \cup U = U$
16. $A \cap \complement A = \emptyset$
17. $A \subset \complement B \rightarrow B \subset \complement A$
18. $A \cup A = A$
19. $A \cap A = A$
20. $A \subset B \leftrightarrow A \cup B = B$ Hint: Start with $A \cup B = B$ and try to find a helpful tautology.
21. $A \subset B \leftrightarrow A \cap B = A$
22. $A \subset \emptyset \leftrightarrow A = \emptyset$
23. If $A \subset B$ and $B \subset C$, then $A \subset C$
24. If $A \subset B$, then $A \cup C \subset B \cup C$

Definition. $A - B = \{x \mid x \in A \wedge x \notin B\} = A \cap \complement B$ = the difference of A and B.

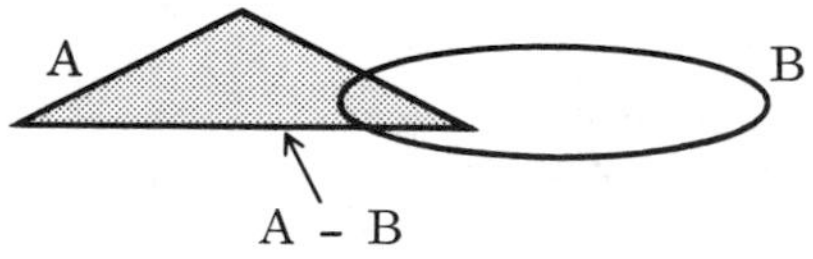

25. $A - \emptyset = A$ Hint: Use Exercise 10 and 15.
26. $A - A = \emptyset$
27. $A \subset B \rightarrow B - (B - A) = A$
28. $(A - B) - C = (A - C) - B$
29. $A - (B - C) = A \cap (\complement B \cup C)$
30. Let I = the set of integers. Show that $\forall A \forall B$, $A - B = B - A$ is false by finding two sets in I for which $A - B \neq B - A$.

Definition. $A \triangle B = \{x \mid x \in A \cup B \wedge x \notin A \cap B\}$
$= (A \cup B) - (A \cap B)$
= the symmetric difference of A and B.

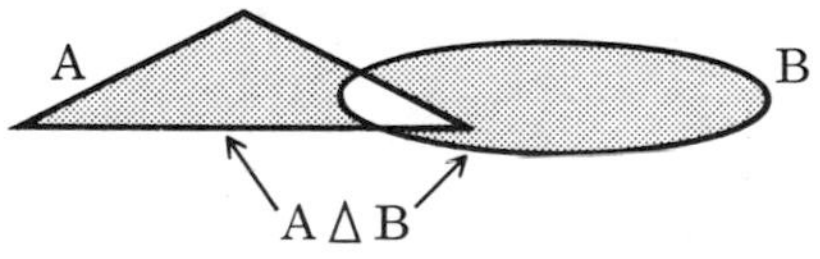

31. $A \triangle B = B \triangle A$
32. $A \triangle B \triangle C = A \triangle (B \triangle C)$
33. $A \cap (B \triangle C) = (A \cap B) \triangle (A \cap C)$
34. $A \triangle B = (A - B) \cup (B - A)$
35. $A \cap B = \emptyset \rightarrow A \triangle B = A \cup B$
36. $A \cup B = (A \triangle B) \triangle (A \cup B)$
37. For any n sets, $n \in N$, $A_1, \ldots, A_n$ we define

$$\bigcup_{i=1}^{n} A_i = \{ x \mid \exists i \in \{1,\ldots,n\} \text{ such that } x \in A_i \};$$

that is, $x \in \bigcup_{i=1}^{n} A_i \leftrightarrow \exists i \in \{1,\ldots,n\},\ x \in A_i$

Also,

$$\bigcap_{i=1}^{n} A_i = \{ x \mid \forall i \{1,\ldots,n\},\ x \in A_i \};$$

that is, $x \in \bigcap_{i=1}^{n} A_i \leftrightarrow \forall i \in \{1,\ldots,n\},\ x \in A_i$

Prove: a) $\bigcup_{i=1}^{n} A_i = (\bigcup_{i=1}^{n-1} A_i) \cup A_n$

b) $\bigcap_{i=1}^{n} A_i = (\bigcap_{i=1}^{n-1} A_i) \cap A_n$

ANSWERS:

Brief proofs are provided, often just an analysis.

1. $x \in A \rightarrow x \in A$, by the tautology $P \rightarrow P$.
2. ANALYSIS: The proof is analogous to the proof of Theorem 4.
3. Using $\leftrightarrow$, string.

$A \subset B \leftrightarrow \forall x(x \in A \rightarrow x \in B)$, by Definition 1
$\leftrightarrow \forall x(x \notin A \vee x \in B)$, by tautology $(P \rightarrow Q) \leftrightarrow (\sim P \vee Q)$
$\leftrightarrow \forall x(x \in \complement A \vee x \in B)$, by Definition 4
$\leftrightarrow \forall x(x \in \complement A \cup B)$, by Definition 2
$\leftrightarrow \complement A \cup B = U$, by Axiom 2.

4. ANALYSIS: Analogous to Theorem 10.
5. ANALYSIS: Analogous to Theorem 9.
6. ANALYSIS: Note the similarity of $A \cup (B \cup C) = (A \cup B) \cup C$ to $P \vee (Q \vee R) \leftrightarrow (P \vee Q) \vee R$.
7. ANALYSIS: Analogous to Exercise 6.
8. $A \subset A \cup \emptyset$ by Theorem 10. To prove $A \cup \emptyset \quad A$ note that

$x \in A \cup \emptyset \rightarrow x \in A \vee x \in \emptyset$.

Now $x \in \emptyset$ is false; that is $x \notin \emptyset$ is true. Then via the tautology $[(P \vee Q) \wedge \sim Q] \to P$ we have $x \in A$. Therefore $A \subset A \cup \emptyset \wedge A \cup \emptyset \subset A$ so $A \cup \emptyset = A$ by Theorem 2.

9. $x \in A \vee x \notin A$, always true by the tautology $P \vee \sim P$.
$\to x \in A \vee x \in \complement A$ for every x
$\to \forall x(x \in A \vee x \in \complement A)$
$\to \forall x(x \in A \cup \complement A)$, by Definition 2.
$\to A \cup \complement A = U$, by Axiom 2.

10. $\forall x(x \notin \emptyset)$, by Axiom 3
$\leftrightarrow \forall x(x \in \complement \emptyset)$, by Definition 4
$\leftrightarrow \complement \emptyset = U$, by Axiom 2.

14. To prove $\forall x(x \in A \to x \in U)$. Consider

$$\underbrace{\underbrace{x \in A}_{F} \to \underbrace{x \in U}_{\text{always true}}}_{\text{T, by definition of '}\to\text{'}} \qquad \underbrace{\underbrace{x \in A}_{T} \to \underbrace{x \in U}_{\text{always true}}}_{\text{T, by definition of '}\to\text{'}}$$

17. ANALYSIS: Use Theorem 11 and Theorem 5.

20. $A \cup B = B \leftrightarrow \forall x(x \in A \cup B \leftrightarrow x \in B)$, by Axiom 1
$\leftrightarrow \forall x[(x \in A \vee x \in B) \leftrightarrow x \in B]$, by Definition 2
$\leftrightarrow \forall x(x \in A \to x \in B)$, by the tautology $[(P \vee Q) \leftrightarrow Q] \leftrightarrow (P \to Q)$
$\leftrightarrow A \subset B$, by Definition 1.

21. ANALYSIS: Analogous to Exercise 20.

22. ANALYSIS: Use Theorems 2 and 3.

23. $A - \emptyset = A \cap \complement \emptyset = A \cap U = A$

27. $B - (B - A) = B \cap \complement(B \cap \complement A)$
$= B \cap (\complement B \cup A)$
$= (B \cap \complement B) \cup (B \cap A)$
$= \emptyset \cup (B \cap A)$
$= B \cap A$

Now $A \subset B \to B \cap A = A$. Hence $A \subset B \to B - (B - A) = A$.

30. Let $A = \{1, 2, 3\}$ and $B = \{2, 3, 4\}$.

32. ANALYSIS: Use Exercise 2 and Theorem 4.

....

PROOF BY CASES

Proof by cases is used several ways and involves the connective '$\vee$'.

<u>Proving a Sentence of the Type $(P \vee R) \to Q$.</u> This type of proof utilizes the tautology

$$[(P \to Q) \wedge (R \to Q)] \to [(P \vee R) \to Q] \qquad (1)$$

The proof is accomplished by proving the antecedent of (1),

$$(P \to Q) \wedge (R \to Q).$$

Hence $(P \to Q)$ and $(R \to Q)$ must be proved. Any mode of proof for conditional sentences can be used. Intuitively*, you want to prove that Q can be deduced from either P or R, so you must show that from either one you can deduce Q.

EXAMPLE. Prove: $(a = 0 \vee b = 0) \rightarrow ab = 0$.

Proof. CASE 1) Prove $a = 0 \rightarrow ab = 0$. Assume $a = 0$. Then $ab = 0 \cdot b = 0$, by P3.
CASE 2) Prove $b = 0 \rightarrow ab = 0$. The proof is analogous to Case 1.●

Similarly, a proof by cases of

$$(P_1 \vee \dots \vee P_n) \rightarrow Q$$

is accomplished by proving

$$\begin{aligned} &P_1 \rightarrow Q \\ &P_2 \rightarrow Q \\ &\quad\vdots \\ &P_n \rightarrow Q. \end{aligned}$$

EXERCISES

1. What tautology justifies this? ______________________
2. There would be ______ cases in such a proof.

ANSWERS:

1. $[(P_1 \rightarrow Q) \wedge \dots \wedge (P_n \rightarrow Q)] \rightarrow [P_1 \vee \dots \vee P_n) \rightarrow Q]$
2. n

....

As an Intermediary Step. Suppose we are again proving

$$P \rightarrow Q.$$

We might discover that

$$P \rightarrow (P_1 \vee P_2 \vee \dots \vee P_n)$$

and

$$(P_1 \rightarrow Q) \wedge (P_2 \rightarrow Q) \wedge \dots \wedge (P_n \rightarrow Q).$$

By proof by cases we have shown that

$$(P_1 \vee P_2 \vee \dots \vee P_n) \rightarrow Q.$$

Then

$$P \rightarrow (P_1 \vee P_2 \vee \dots \vee P_n)$$

and

$$(P_1 \vee P_2 \vee \dots \vee P_n) \rightarrow Q$$

* Which means "appealling to your mathematical experience".

implies by the Law of Syllogism, that

$P \rightarrow Q$.

Hence another way to use proof by cases is as an intermediary step derived from the antecedent of a conditional sentence.

EXAMPLE. Recall the definition: $|x| = x$ when $x \geq 0$

$|x| = -x$ when $x < 0$.

Prove: If x is a real number, then $|x| \geq 0$.

Proof. If x is a real number, then $x \geq 0 \lor x < 0$. Prove

$(x \geq 0 \lor x < 0) \rightarrow |x| \geq 0$.

CASE 1) $x \geq 0$. If $x \geq 0$, then by definition $|x| = x$ so $|x| \geq 0$.

CASE 2) $x < 0$. If $x < 0$, then by definition $|x| = -x$. By properties of inequalities if $x < 0$, then $-x > 0$ so $|x| > 0$.

Hence $(x \geq 0 \lor x < 0) \rightarrow |x| \geq 0$. Therefore, if x is a real number, then $|x| \geq 0$. ●

The art of producing a proof by cases may be discovering what set of exhaustive cases is appropriate. For example, if x is a real number you might use

a) $x \geq 0 \lor x < 0$
b) $x > 0 \lor x = 0 \lor x < 0$
c) $x > 2 \lor x = 2 \lor x < 2$

EXERCISES

Complete.

1. If A is an angle, the cases you might consider are

   A acute $\lor$ ______________ $\lor$ ________________

2. If f is a function the cases you might consider are

   a) f is differentiable $\lor$ ________________
   b) f is even $\lor$ ___________ $\lor$ f is neither even nor odd.
   c) f is constant $\lor$ ________________

3. If x is an integer the cases you might consider are

   a) x is even $\lor$ __________
   b) $x > 9 \lor$ _____________ $\lor\ x < 9$

ANSWERS:

1. A right; A oblique
2. a) f is not differentiable
   b) f is odd
   c) f is not constant

3. a) x is odd
   b) x = 9

....

Notice that each of the previous lists is exhaustive in that all possibilities occurred. For example, a function is either differentable or not differentiable, an integer is either odd or even, nothing else.

EXERCISES

Use proof by cases to prove the following.

1. If x is a real number, then $|-x| = |x|$.
2. If x is a real number, then $|x^2| = |x|^2$.
3. For every real number x, $x \leq |x|$.
4. If x and y are real numbers, then $|xy| = |x| \cdot |y|$. Hint: One or both of x, y is zero or both are nonzero.
5. If $a > 0$, then $|x| < a$ iff $-a < x < a$.
6. If $a > 0$, then $|x| > a$ iff $x > a \vee x < -a$.
7. If x and y are real numbers, then $|x + y| \leq |x| + |y|$.
8. If x and y are real numbers, then $|x| - |y| \leq |x - y|$.
9. If f is a strictly monotone function, then f is one-to-one. Hint: f is strictly monotone $\rightarrow$ f is strictly increasing or strictly decreasing.
10. If x is an integer, then $x^2 - x$ is even.
11. If x is an integer, then $x^2 + x + 1$ is odd.
12. Find a proof by cases of the Law of Cosines in a trigonometry book. Explain the use of proof by cases.
13. Find a proof by cases of the formula

    $$\sin(a + b) = \sin a \cos b + \cos a \sin b$$

    in a trigonometry book. Explain the use of proof by cases.
14. Find a proof by cases of Rolle's Theorem in a calculus book. Explain the use of proof by cases.
15. The function g described by $g(x) = |x|$, $x \neq 0$, is differentiable while the function f described by $f(x) = |x|$ is not differentiable. Find a formula for g' using proof by cases. Use a calculus book if necessary.
16. Suppose P(x) and Q(x) are statements for each x in a universal set U. Prove

    $$\{x \mid P(x) \vee Q(x)\} = \{x \mid P(x)\} \cup \{x \mid Q(x)\}.$$

17. Prove: Every sentence of the type

    $$[\forall x P(x) \vee \forall x Q(x)] \rightarrow [\forall x, P(x) \vee Q(x)]$$

    is true.
18. Suppose you want to prove a sentence of the type

    $$P \rightarrow (R \wedge Q)$$

    by contrapositive. Explain the possible role of proof by cases in such a proof.

ANSWERS:

1. $x \text{ real} \to x > 0 \vee x < 0 \vee x = 0$

   CASE 1) $x > 0 \to |x| = x$
   $x > 0 \to -x < 0 \to |-x| = -(-x) = x$
   $\therefore |-x| = |x|$

   CASE 2) $x < 0 \to |x| = -x$
   $x < 0 \to -x > 0 \to |-x| = -x$
   $\therefore |-x| = |x|$

   CASE 3) $x = 0 \to |x| = x$
   $x = 0 \to -x = 0 \to |-x| = 0 = x$
   $\therefore |-x| = |x|$

2. $x \text{ real} \to x \geq 0 \vee x < 0$

   CASE 1) $x \geq 0 \to x^2 \geq 0 \to |x^2| = x^2$

   $x \geq 0 \to |x| = x \to |x|^2 = x^2$

   $\therefore |x|^2 = |x^2|$

   CASE 2) $x < 0 \to x^2 > 0 \to |x^2| = x^2$

   $x < 0 \to |x| = -x \to |x|^2 = (-x)(-x) = x^2$

   $\therefore |x^2| = |x|^2$

10. x is an integer $\to$ x is even or x is odd

    CASE 1) x is even. Then $x = 2k$ for some $k \in I$.
    Hence $x^2 - x = (2k)^2 - (2k) = 4k^2 - 2k = 2(2k^2 - k)$,
    so $x^2 - x$ is even

    CASE 2) x is odd. Then $x = 2k + 1$ for some $k \in I$. You complete.

11. ANALYSIS: Analogous to Exercise 9.
15. $x \neq 0 \to x > 0$ or $x < 0$

    CASE 1) $x > 0 \to f(x) = |x| = x \to f'(x) = 1$

    CASE 2) $x < 0 \to f(x) = |x| = -x \to f'(x) = -1$

....

MATHEMATICAL INDUCTION

Consider proving sentences of the type

For every natural number n, P(n)

or

$\forall n P(n)$,

where the quantifier refers to the universal set $N = \{1, 2, 3, \ldots\}$. One way to prove sentences of this type is by <u>mathematical induction</u> which uses a rule of reasoning not yet discussed. The following is the mathematical induction sentence which the mathematician accepts as an axiom. [This is another situation in which the mathematician makes assumptions about how he will reason.]

$$P(1) \wedge \forall k[P(k) \rightarrow P(k+1)] \rightarrow \forall n P(n) \qquad \text{(MI)}$$

If we can prove the antecedent of MI,

$$P(1) \wedge \forall k[P(k) \rightarrow P(k+1),$$

then by modus ponens we can deduce

$$\forall n P(n).$$

Thus there are two steps in the proof of $\forall n P(n)$;

1) BASIS STEP. Prove $P(1)$
2) INDUCTION STEP. Prove $\forall k[P(k) \rightarrow P(k+1)]$

That is, we prove $P(1)$ and for every k, $P(k) \rightarrow P(k+1)$.

To explain intuitively how this proves $\forall n P(n)$ suppose we have completed both parts of the induction proof; that is $P(1)$ and $\forall k[P(k) \rightarrow P(k+1)]$ are proved. We have deduced an endless sequence of sentences

$$\begin{array}{l} P(1) \\ \left.\begin{array}{l} P(1) \rightarrow P(2) \\ P(2) \rightarrow P(3) \\ \vdots \\ P(n-1) \rightarrow P(n) \\ \vdots \end{array}\right\} \quad \forall k[P(k) \rightarrow P(k+1)] \end{array}$$

The process then becomes similar to knocking over a row of tin soldiers for

$$\begin{array}{l} P(1) \\ \underline{P(1) \rightarrow P(2)} \\ \therefore P(2) \end{array}, \text{ then } \begin{array}{l} P(2) \\ \underline{P(2) \rightarrow P(3)} \\ \therefore P(3) \end{array}, \text{ then } \begin{array}{l} P(3) \\ \underline{P(3) \rightarrow P(4)} \\ \therefore P(4) \end{array}, \text{ and so on,}$$

producing the endless sequence

$$P(1), P(2), \ldots, P(n), \ldots;$$

that is, we have proved

$$\forall n P(n).$$

EXAMPLE. Prove $\forall n, 2^n < 2^{n+1}$

Proof. $P(n)$: $2^n < 2^{n+1}$

1) BASIS STEP: Prove $P(1)$: $2^1 < 2^{1+1}$
   Now $2^1 = 2$, $2^{1+1} = 4$, so $2^1 < 2^{1+1}$.
2) INDUCTION STEP: Prove $\forall k[P(k) \rightarrow P(k+1)]$

Assume P(k): $2^k < 2^{k+1}$

Deduce P(k+1): $2^{k+1} < 2^{k+2}$

Since $2^k < 2^{k+1}$, $2^k \cdot 2 < 2^{k+1} \cdot 2$, or $2^{k+1} < 2^{k+2}$; that is P(k + 1).●
ANALYSIS: We saw that multiplying both sides of the inequality P(k) by 2 gave the inequality P(k + 1).

When doing a proof by mathematical induction it is helpful to list

P(n),
P(1),
P(k),
P(k + 1)

as illustrated in the previous example. This aids in identifying what is to be assumed and what is to be proved. Usually proving P(1) is just a matter of substitution, but proving $\forall k[P(k) \rightarrow P(k+1)]$ requires more effort. An aid to doing this is having listed P(k) and P(k + 1), examine P(k + 1) and try to discover some way of deriving it from P(k).

EXAMPLE. <u>Prove:</u> For every natural number n,

$$D^n(xe^x) = (x + n)e^x.$$

['D^n' represents the n'th derivative with respect to x.]

<u>Proof.</u> P(n): $D^n(xe^x) = (x + n)e^x$

1) BASIS STEP. Prove P(1): $D(xe^x) = (x + 1)e^x$

Using the product rule for derivatives we have

$$D(xe^x) = xe^x + e^x = (x + 1)e^x,$$

so P(1) is true.

2) INDUCTION STEP. Prove $\forall k[P(k) \rightarrow P(k+1)]$

Assume P(k): $D^k(xe^x) = (x + k)e^x$

Deduce P(k + 1): $D^{k+1}(xe^x) = [x + (k+1)]e^x$.

Now $D^{k+1}(xe^x) = D[D^k(xe^x)]$, since from calculus we know $D^{k+1} = D(D^k)$.

$= D[(x + k)e^x]$, by P(k)

$= (x + k)e^x + e^x$, by the product rule for derivatives

$= [x + (k + 1)]e^x$

Hence P(k + 1).●
ANALYSIS: The trick was to recall that $D^{k+1}(xe^x) = D[D^k(xe^x)]$ and then substitute via P(k).

It is important to realize that mathematical induction can be applied to prove any sentence $\forall n P(n)$ which refers to the natural numbers. Whether the proof can be accomplished is another problem. We give some further examples.

EXAMPLE. Prove for every n sets, $n \in N$, $A_1, \ldots, A_n$,

$$\mathcal{C}\left(\bigcup_{i=1}^{n} A_i\right) = \bigcap_{i=1}^{n} \mathcal{C}A_i$$

<u>Proof:</u> $P(n)$: $\mathcal{C}\left(\bigcup_{i=1}^{n} A_i\right) = \bigcap_{i=1}^{n} \mathcal{C}A_i$

1) BASIS STEP. Prove $P(1)$: $\mathcal{C}(A_1) = \mathcal{C}A_1$.

Nothing to prove

2) INDUCTION STEP. Prove $\forall k[\,P(k) \rightarrow P(k+1)\,]$

Assume $P(k)$: $\mathcal{C}\left(\bigcup_{i=1}^{k} A_i\right) = \bigcap_{i=1}^{k} \mathcal{C}A_i$

Deduce $P(k+1)$: $\mathcal{C}\left(\bigcup_{i=1}^{k+1} A_i\right) = \bigcap_{i=1}^{k+1} \mathcal{C}A_i$

Now $\mathcal{C}\left(\bigcup_{i=1}^{k+1} A_i\right) = \mathcal{C}\left[\left(\bigcup_{i=1}^{k} A_i\right) \quad A_{k+1}\right]$

$= \mathcal{C}\left(\bigcup_{i=1}^{k} A_i\right) \cap \mathcal{C}A_{k+1}$, by $\mathcal{C}(A \cup B) = \mathcal{C}A \cap \mathcal{C}B$

where we consider $\bigcup_{i=1}^{k} A_i$ to be one set and A_{k+1} to be the other.

$= \left(\bigcap_{i=1}^{k} \mathcal{C}A_i\right) \cap \mathcal{C}A_{k+1}$, by $P(k)$

$= \bigcap_{i=1}^{k+1} A_i$. ●

That both the basis and induction steps are essential in a proof by mathematical induction is evidenced in the following examples. There are sentences $P(n)$ for which

$P(1)$ is true

but

$\forall n P(n)$ and $\forall k[\,P(k) \rightarrow P(k+1)\,]$ are <u>false</u>.

EXAMPLE. Consider $P(n)$: $n^2 = n$.

EXERCISES

1. Prove $\forall n P(n)$ is false by finding a counterexample.
2. Prove $P(1)$.
3. Form the negation of $\forall k[\,P(k) \rightarrow P(k+1)\,]$ ____________________.
   Prove the negation.

ANSWERS:

1. $2^2 \neq 2$ 2. $1^2 = 1$
3. $\exists k[\ P(k) \wedge \sim P(k+1)\ ]$, or $\exists k,\ k^2 = k \wedge (k+1)^2 \neq k+1$.

   Let $k = 1$
   Then $1^2 = 1 \wedge (1+1)^2 \neq 1+1$.

....

There are sentences P(n) for which

$\forall k[\ P(k) \rightarrow P(k+1)\ ]$ is true

but

P(1) and $\forall n P(n)$ are false.

EXAMPLE. Consider P(n): $n = n + 1$

EXERCISES

1. Prove $\forall n P(n)$ is false by finding a counterexample.
2. Prove P(1) false.
3. Prove $\forall k[\ P(k) \rightarrow P(k+1)\ ]$

ANSWERS:

1. $1 \neq 1 + 1$ 2. $1 \neq 1 + 1$
3. Assume P(k): $k = k + 1$
   Deduce P(k + 1): $k + 1 = k + 2$
   Adding 1 to both sides of

   $k = k + 1$

   we have

   $k + 1 = k + 2$

....

In the previous example we could line up the tin soldiers but we could not knock over the first one.

Mathematical induction can also be used to prove sentences referring to certain subsets of the integers. For any universal set of the type

$\{\ x \mid x \in I \text{ and } x \geq h, \text{ for some fixed } h \in I\}$

the following rule of reasoning may be used:

$$\{\ P(h) \wedge \underset{k \geq h}{\forall k}[\ P(k) \rightarrow P(k+1)\ ]\ \} \rightarrow \forall x P(x) \qquad \text{(MI')}$$

Examples of sets for which this induction can be applied are the following:

$\{\ -3, -2, -1, 0, 1, 2, 3, \ldots\}$,
$\{\ 5, 6, 7, \ldots\}$,
$\{\ 0, 1, 2, \ldots\}$.

This is illustrated in subsequent example.

EXERCISES

Complete

1. $\emptyset$ has 0 elements; $\mathcal{P}(\emptyset)$ has ________ elements.
2. $\{a\}$ has 1 element; $\mathcal{P}(\{a\})$ has ________ elements.
3. $\{a, b\}$ has 2 elements; $\mathcal{P}(\{a, b\})$ has ________ elements.
4. $\{a, b, c\}$ has 3 elements; $\mathcal{P}(\{a, b, c\})$ has ________ elements.
5. Suppose A has n elements. Conjecture a formula for the number of elements in $\mathcal{P}(A)$. ________

ANSWERS:

1. 1 2. 2 3. 4 4. 8 5. 2^n

....

EXAMPLE. Prove: For every finite set A and for every $n \geq 0$, if A has n elements, then $\mathcal{P}(A)$ has 2^n elements.

Proof. Let A be an arbitrary finite set. Consider

$P(n)$: A has n elements $\rightarrow \mathcal{P}(A)$ has 2^n elements

1) BASIS STEP. Prove $P(0)$:

A has 0 elements $\rightarrow \mathcal{P}(A)$ has 2^0 elements

Now

$$\begin{aligned} \text{A has 0 elements} &\rightarrow A = \emptyset \\ &\rightarrow \mathcal{P}(A) = \{\emptyset\} \\ &\rightarrow \mathcal{P}(A) \text{ has 1, or } 2^0 \text{ elements} \end{aligned}$$

2) INDUCTION STEP.

Assume $P(k)$: A has k elements $\rightarrow \mathcal{P}(A)$ has 2^k elements

Deduce $P(k+1)$: A has $k + 1$ elements $\rightarrow \mathcal{P}(A)$ has 2^{k+1} elements.

Notice that $P(k)$ is of the form $P \rightarrow Q$ and $P(k+1)$ is of the form $S \rightarrow R$; we are trying to prove $(P \rightarrow Q) \rightarrow (S \rightarrow R)$. In a previous exercise set we discussed proving this type of sentence via the tautology

$$[(P \rightarrow Q) \rightarrow (S \rightarrow R)] \leftrightarrow [(P \rightarrow Q) \wedge S) \rightarrow R].$$

Hence we assume $P(k)$ and that A has $k + 1$ elements. Then A could be described by

$$\begin{aligned} A &= \{a_1, a_2, \ldots, a_k, a_{k+1}\} \\ &= \{a_1, a_2, \ldots, a_k\} \cup \{a_{k+1}\} \end{aligned}$$

Consider the set $A' = \{a_1, \ldots, a_k\}$. Every subset of A' is a subset of A.

EXERCISES

1. a) How many elements has $\wp(A')$? ______________
   b) Why?
2. Suppose we add the element a_{k+1} to each subset of A'. How many new subsets of A do we obtain? ______________

ANSWERS:

1. a) 2^k b) by P(k)
2. 2^k

. . . .

Convince yourself that there are no other subsets of A. Since A' has 2^k subsets and we found 2^k more, there are

$$\begin{aligned} 2^k + 2^k &= 2(2^k) \\ &= 2^{k+1} \text{ subsets of A} \end{aligned}$$

That is, $\wp(A)$ has 2^{k+1} elements. ●

EXERCISES

Prove the following by mathematical induction.

1. $\forall n \in N,\ 2^n > n.$
2. $\forall n \in N,\ 3^n > n.$
3. $\forall n \in N,\ 2 \leq 2^n$
4. $\forall n \in N,\ 2n \leq 2^n$ Hint: Use Exercise 3.
5. $\forall n \in N,\ n < n+1.$
6. $\forall n \in N,\ 2^{n-1} \leq n!$ Hint: $(k+1) = (k+1)k$
7. $\forall n \geq 4,\ 2^n < n!$ Prove $2^n < n$ false when $n = 3$.
8. Let a and b be real numbers.
   Prove: $\forall n \in N(a < b \rightarrow a^n < b^n).$
9. $\forall n \in N,\ (2n)! < 2^{2n}(n!)^2.$
10. $\forall n \in N,\ |\sin(nx)| \leq n\,|\sin x|$. Hint: Use $\sin(a+b) = \sin a \cos b + \cos a \sin b$.
11. <u>DeMoivre's Theorem</u>: $\forall n \in N, \forall n \in R,$
    $(\cos u + i \sin u)^n = \cos(nu) + i \sin(nu),\ i^2 = -1.$
12. $\forall n \in N,\ \cos u \cdot \cos 2u \cdots \cos 2^{n-1}u = \dfrac{\sin 2^n u}{2^n \sin u},\ \sin u \neq 0.$
13. <u>Bernoulli's Inequality</u>:
    $a > 1 \rightarrow \forall n \in N,\ (1 + a)^n \geq 1 + an.$

14. $\forall n \in N$, $D(x^n) = nx^{n-1}$. Hint: assume $x^o = 1$ and use the product rule for derivatives.

15. $\forall n \in N$, $D^n(\log_e x) = (-1)^n (n-1)!\, x^{-n}$.

16. $\forall n \geq 5$, $2^n > n^2$.

17. $\forall n \geq 6$, $n^3 < n!$

18. For every n sets, $n \in N$, $A_1, \ldots, A_n$

$$C\left(\bigcap_{i=1}^{n} A_i\right) = \bigcup_{i=1}^{n} C A_i$$

19. $\forall n \in N$, $\sum_{j=1}^{n} j = (n^2 + n)/2$; that is, $1 + 2 + \ldots + n = (n^2 + n)/2$.

20. $\forall n \in N$, $\sum_{j=2}^{n} \frac{1}{\sqrt{j}} > \sqrt{n}$

21. $\forall n \in N$, $\sum_{j=1}^{n} j^2 = \frac{n(n+1)(2n+1)}{6}$

22. $\forall n \in N$, $\sum_{j=1}^{n} \frac{1}{j(j+1)} = \frac{n}{n+1}$

23. $\forall n \in N$, $\sum_{j=1}^{n} 2^j = 2^{n+1} - 2$

24. $\forall n \in N$, $\sum_{j=1}^{n} j \cdot j! = (n+1)! - 1$

25. $\forall n \in N$, $\sum_{j=1}^{n} j(j+1) = \frac{n(n+1)(n+2)}{3}$

26. $\forall n \in N$, $\sum_{j=1}^{n} \frac{j}{(j+1)!} = 1 - \frac{1}{(n+1)!}$

27. $\forall n \in N, \sum_{j=1}^{n} j^3 = \frac{n^4 + 2n^2 + n^2}{2}$

28. Given the real numbers $a_1, \ldots, a_n$ and using $|x+y| \leq |x| + |y|$,

prove $|\sum_{i=1}^{n} a_i| \leq \sum_{i=1}^{n} |a_i|$.

29. Given a set of n points in the plane, $n \geq 2$, no three of which are collinear. Prove that the number of straight lines joining these points is $n(n-1)/2$.

30. $\forall m \geq 2 \forall n \in N, m^n > n$. Hint: $m \geq 2$ be arbitrary. Then prove $\forall n \in N, m^n > n$ by MI.

31. $\forall n \in N, 1 + r + r^2 + \ldots + r^{n-1} = \frac{r^n - 1}{r - 1}$ $(r \neq 1)$

This is the formula for the sum of the terms of a geometric progression.

32. $\forall n \in N, a + (a+d) + \ldots + (a + nd) = \frac{1}{2}(n+1)(2a + nd)$

This is the formula for the sum of the terms of an arithmetic progression.

33. Why cannot the following be proved by MI?

a) $\forall n \in N, 3 + 5 + \ldots + (2n + 1) = (n + 1)^2$

b) $\forall n \in N, 1 + 3 + \ldots + (2n - 1) = n^2 + 3$

34. Find the error in this proof.

Theorem. Everyone is of the same sex.

Proof. Let P(n) be the following sentence:

If A is a set containing n people, then all the people have the same sex.

Indeed, P(1) is true. Assume P(k) is true. Let A be a set of k+1 people. Then A is the union of two overlapping sets A_1 and A_2 each containing k people. (Consider the following illustration when n = 5)

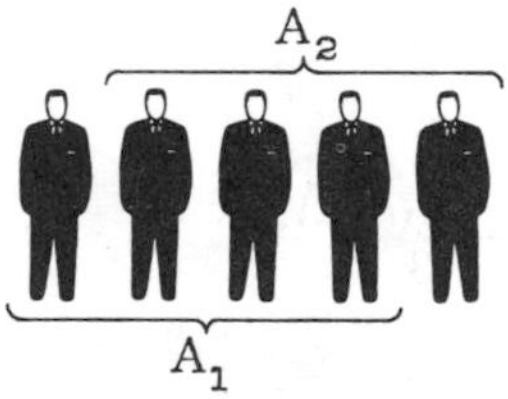

By P(k) all the people in A_1 are of the same sex, and all the people in A_2 are of the same sex. Since A_1 and A_2 overlap all the people in A are of the same sex.

35. Use proof by cases and mathematical induction to prove the following.

For every natural number n, $i^n = 1, -1, i,$ or $-i$, where $i^2 = -1$.

ANSWERS:

In most of these answers only the induction step is given. You should be able to complete the basis step.

1. Assume P(k): $2^k > k$

   Deduce P(k+1): $2^{k+1} > k+1$

   Now $2^{k+1} = 2 \cdot 2^k > 2k$, by P(k)

   $2k = k + k \geq k + 1$, since for every natural number k, $k \geq 1$.

   We used property 03 of the Appendix.

2. ANALYSIS: Analogous to Exercise 1.

3. Assume P(k): $2 \leq 2^k$

   Deduce P(k+1): $2 \leq 2^{k+1}$

   Now $2^{k+1} \geq 2^k$, by an Example.
   ≥ 2, by P(k)

4. Assume P(k): $2k \leq 2^k$

   Deduce P(k+1): $2(k+1) \leq 2^{k+1}$

   Now $2(k+1) = 2k + 2 \leq 2^k + 2$, by P(k)

   $\leq 2^k + 2^k$, by Exercise 3

   $= 2(2^k) = 2^{k+1}$

6. Assume P(k): $2^{k-1} \leq k!$

   Deduce P(k+1): $2^k \leq (k+1)!$

   Now $2^k = 2(2^{k-1}) \leq 2 \cdot k!$, by P(k)

   $\leq (k+1)k!$, since $k \geq 1 \rightarrow k + 1 \geq 1 + 1 = 2$.

   $= (k + 1)!$

7. BASIS STEP. P(4): $2^4 < 4!$

   Now $2^4 = 16$ and $4! = 24$ so $2^4 < 4!$

   INDUCTION STEP.

   Assume P(k): $2^k < k!$

   Deduce P(k+1): $2^{k+1} < (k+1)!$

   $2^{k+1} = 2(2^k) < 2 \cdot k!$, by P(k)

   $\leq (k+1)k!$

   $= (k+1)!$

9. INDUCTION STEP.

Assume P(k): $(2k)! < 2^{2k}(k!)^2$

Deduce P(k+1): $[2(k+1)]! < 2^{2k+2}[(k+1)!]^2$

Now

$$[2(k+1)]! = (2k+2)(2k+1)(2k)! = (4k^2 + 4k + 2)\underline{(2k)!}$$

and

$$\begin{aligned}2^{2k+2}[(k+1)!]^2 &= 2^{2k+2} \cdot [(k+1)(k!)]^2 \\ &= 2^{2k+2} \cdot (k+1)^2 (k!)^2 \\ &= 2^{2k} \cdot 2^2 \cdot (k^2 + 2k + 1)(k!)^2 \\ &= \underline{2^{2k}}(4k^2 + 8k + 4)\underline{(k!)^2}\end{aligned}$$

Then noting that $(4k^2 + 4k + 2) < 4k^2 + 8k + 4$ and using P(k) we have

$$\begin{aligned}[2(k+1)]! &= (4k^2 + 4k + 2)(2k)! \\ &< (4k^2 + 4k + 2) \cdot 2^{2k} \cdot (k!)^2 \text{, by P(k)} \\ &< 2^{2k} \cdot (4k^2 + 8k + 4)(k!)^2 \\ &= 2^{2k+2}[(k+1)!]^2\end{aligned}$$

ANALYSIS: The two expressions of P(k+1) were expanded to hopefully see where P(k) could be applied. Note the underlining. The proof then followed via P(k) and the noted inequality.

10. INDUCTION STEP.

Assume P(k): $|\sin kx| \le k|\sin x|$

Deduce P(k+1): $|\sin (k+1)x| \le (k+1)\,|\sin x|$

Now

$$\begin{aligned}|\sin (k+1)x| &= |\sin(kx+x)| \\ &= |\sin kx \cos x + \cos kx \sin x| \text{, by the formula in the hint.} \\ &\le |\sin kx \cos x| + |\cos kx \sin x| \text{, by } |p+q| \le |p| + |q| \\ &= |\sin kx| \cdot |\cos x| + |\cos kx| \cdot |\sin x| \text{, since } |pq| = |p| \cdot |q| \\ &\le |\sin kx| + |\sin x| \text{, since } |\cos x| \le 1 \text{ and } |\sin x| \le 1 \\ &\le k|\sin x| + |\sin x| \text{, by P(k)} \\ &= (k+1)\,|\sin x|.\end{aligned}$$

12. BASIS STEP. Prove P(1): $\cos u = \dfrac{\sin 2u}{2 \sin u}$

$$\frac{\sin 2u}{2 \sin u} = \frac{2 \sin u \cos u}{2 \sin u} = \cos u$$

INDUCTION STEP.

Assume P(k): $\cos u \cdots \cos 2^{k-1}u = \dfrac{\sin 2^k u}{2^k \sin u}$

Deduce P(k+1): $\cos u \cdots \cos 2^{k-1}u \cos 2^k u = \dfrac{\sin 2^{k+1}u}{2^{k+1}\sin u}$

Now $\cos u \cdots \cos 2^{k-1}u \cdot \cos 2^k u = \dfrac{\sin 2^k u}{2^k \sin u} \cdot \cos 2^k u$ by P(k)

$$= \frac{\sin 2^k u \cdot \cos 2^k u}{2^k \sin u}$$

$$= \frac{1/2 \sin 2(2^k u)}{2^k \sin u}, \text{ since } 2 \sin a \cos a = \sin 2a$$

$$= \frac{\sin 2^{k+1}u}{2^{k+1} \sin u}$$

19. INDUCTION STEP.

Assume P(k): $\sum_{j=1}^{k} j = \dfrac{k^2 + k}{2}$

Deduce P(k+1): $\sum_{j=1}^{k+1} j = \dfrac{(k+1)^2 + (k+1)}{2} = \dfrac{k^2 + 3k + 2}{2}$

Now

$\sum_{j=1}^{k+1} j = \sum_{j=1}^{k} j + (k+1)$, by definition of $\sum$ notation.

$$= \frac{k^2 + k}{2} + (k+1), \text{ by P(k)}$$

$$= \frac{k^2 + k}{2} + \frac{2(k+1)}{2}$$

$$= \frac{k^2 + 3k + 2}{2}$$

21. BASIS STEP. $\sum_{j=1}^{1} j^2 = 1^2 = \dfrac{1 \cdot (1+1) \cdot (2+1)}{6}$

INDUCTION STEP.

Assume P(k): $\sum_{j=1}^{k} j^2 = \frac{k \cdot (k+1) \cdot (2k+1)}{6}$

Deduce P(k+1): $\sum_{j=1}^{k+1} j^2 = \frac{(k+1) \cdot (k+2) \cdot [\,2(k+1) + 1\,]}{6}$

$$= \frac{(k+1) \cdot (k+2) \cdot (2k + 3)}{6}$$

Now

$\sum_{j=1}^{k+1} j^2 = \sum_{j=1}^{k} j^2 + (k+1)^2$, by definition of $\sum$ notation.

$= \frac{k \cdot (k+1) \cdot (2k+1)}{6} + (k+1)^2$, by P(k)

$$= (k+1) \cdot \frac{k \cdot (2k+1)}{6} + (k+1)$$

$$= (k+1) \cdot \frac{k \cdot (2k+1)}{6} + \frac{6(k+1)}{6}$$

$$= (k+1) \cdot \frac{2k^2 + k + 6k + 6}{6}$$

$$= (k+1) \cdot \frac{2k^2 + 7k + 6}{6}$$

$$= \frac{(k+1) \cdot (k+2) \cdot (2k+3)}{6}$$

34. Test the argument when proving $P(1) \rightarrow P(2)$.

....

PROOF BY CONTRADICTION

"Eliminate all other factors, and the one which remains must be the truth." [Sherlock Holmes]

Sir Arthur Conan Doyle, The Sign of Four

A contradiction is a statement which is false no matter what the truth value of its constituent parts. For example, the sentence

$R \wedge \sim R$

is always false.

EXERCISE

Complete this truth table.

R	$\sim R$	$R \wedge \sim R$
T	F	
F	T	

ANSWERS:

F, F

A proof by contradiction of a sentence

P

is a proof that assumes

$\sim P$

and yields a sentence of the type

$R \wedge \sim R,$

where R is any sentence including P, an axiom, or any previously proved theorem. This is justified by the tautology

$$[\sim P \wedge (R \wedge \sim R)] \rightarrow P$$

Intuitively, P can only be true or false, but not both. If we assume its negation true and this yields another sentence both true and false then $\sim P$ cannot be true so P must be true.

The phrases reductio ad absurdum, meaning "reduce to an absurdity", and indirect proof also refer to proof by contradiction.

The importance of being able to form sentence negations is realized when doing proofs by contradiction. To begin such proofs you must know how to form negations.

EXERCISES

What would you assume to begin a proof by contradiction of the following?

1. $\forall x\, P(x)$ 2. $\exists x\, P(x)$ 3. $P \rightarrow Q$ 4. $Q \rightarrow \exists x\, P(x)$

ANSWERS:

1. $\exists x \sim P(x)$ 2. $\forall x \sim P(x)$ 3. $P \wedge \sim Q$ 4. $Q \wedge \forall x \sim P(x)$

Proof by contradiction provides another mode of proof for proving sentences of the type

$\forall x\, P(x)$

or

$\exists x\ P(x)$

In fact, it provides another mode of proof for proving any sentence.

We proved several sentences of the type $\exists x\ P(x)$ directly, by displaying an x such that P(x) is true. A proof by contradiction of $\exists x\ P(x)$ may not display an x; that is, one could prove there exists an x without displaying it. This is illustrated in calculus where an indirect proof* of the sentence

$$\exists x, \lim_{n \to \infty} \int_1^n e^{-y^2}\, dy = x$$

can be given without actually displaying x.

Proofs of existence theorems in differential equations provide other such illustrations.

Proving a Sentence of the Type $P \to Q$ by Contradiction. Most proofs by contradiction are of sentences of the type $P \to Q$. To prove a sentence of the type

$$P \to Q$$

by contradiction, assume its negation

$$\sim (P \to Q)$$

or

$$P \wedge \sim Q.$$

Hence assume both P and $\sim Q$ true.

EXAMPLE. Prove: $x \neq 0 \to x^{-1} \neq 0$

Proof. For contradiction assume the negation

$$x \neq 0 \wedge x^{-1} = 0$$

Then by M4,

$$x \cdot x^{-1} = 1$$

Also, using $x^{-1} = 0$ and P3,

$$x \cdot x^{-1} = x \cdot 0 = 0.$$

Hence $1 = 0$. Thus the contradiction is

$$1 \neq 0 \wedge 1 = 0$$

So

$$x \neq 0 \to x^{-1} \neq 0. \bullet$$

---

* See Thomas, George B. Calculus and Analytic Geometry, Reading, Mass., Addison-Wesley Pub. Co., 4th Ed., 1968, p. 307.

EXAMPLE. Prove:

If x is rational and y is irrational, then x + y is irrational.

Proof. The sentence is of the type

$$(P \wedge Q) \to R$$

where

P: x is rational
Q: y is irrational
R: x + y is irrational

For contradiction, assume

$$\sim [(P \wedge Q) \to R]$$

or

$$(P \wedge Q) \wedge \sim R.$$

That is, assume

x is rational
y is irrational
x + y is not irrational (rational)

Since x and x+y are rational,

$$x = \frac{a}{b}, \text{ for some integer a and b}$$

$$x + y = \frac{c}{d}, \text{ for some integers c and d.}$$

Then

$$(x + y) - x = \frac{c}{d} - \frac{a}{b}$$

$$= \frac{cb - da}{db}$$

Since ab - da and db are both integers

(x + y) - x is a rational number

But

$$(x + y) - x = y,$$

so y is rational. That is,

$$\sim Q: \sim (\text{y is irrational}).$$

Hence we have $Q \wedge \sim Q$, a contradiction. Thus we have proved $(P \wedge Q) \to R$. ●

Let us compare three modes of proof for proving sentences of the type $P \to Q$. Suppose $S_1, \ldots, S_n$ are the axioms and previously proved theorems.

RCP:

$$S_1, \ldots, S_n, P \vdash Q$$

Contrapositive:

$$S_1, \ldots, S_n, \sim Q \vdash \sim P$$

Contradiction:

$$S_1, \ldots, S_n, P, \sim Q \vdash R \wedge \sim R$$

EXAMPLES. These are examples of contradiction proofs.

$$S_1, \ldots, S_n, P, \sim Q \vdash P \wedge \sim P$$

$$S_1, \ldots, S_n, P, \sim Q \vdash Q \wedge \sim Q$$

$$S_1, \ldots, S_n, P, \sim Q \vdash S_i \wedge \sim S_i, \; S_i \in \{S_1, \ldots, S_n\}$$

Comparing we see that with RCP we assume P with the explicit intention of deducing Q. With the contrapositive we assume $\sim Q$ with the explicit intention of deducing $\sim P$. But in using proof by contradiction we assume both P and $\sim Q$ and try to deduce any sentence R and its negation $\sim R$. $\sim R$ could be $\sim P$, Q, $\sim S_i$ for some known fact S_i, or could be some sentence and its negation deduced from $S_1, \ldots, S_n$, P, and $\sim Q$.

Proof by contrapositive and proof by contradiction with conclusion $\sim P$ are similar but a proof by contradiction assumes P while proof by contrapositive does not.

EXERCISES

1. In the proof of

   $$x \neq 0 \rightarrow x^{-1} \neq 0$$

   is the contradiction of a previously known fact or of a constituent part of the sentence?
2. In the proof of

   If x is rational and y is irrational, then x + y is irrational.

   is the contradiction of a previously known fact or of a constituent part of the sentence?

ANSWERS:

1. known fact 2. constituent part of sentence

....

EXAMPLE. Suppose f is a function.

Prove: If for every $p > 0$ and every x, $f(x+p) = f(x)$, then f is constant. (1)

EXERCISES

1. Translate sentence (1) to logical symbolism.
2. Form the negation of sentence (1).

ANSWERS:

1. $[\forall p > 0 \, \forall x, \, f(x+p) = f(x)] \rightarrow f$ is constant.
2. $[\forall p > 0 \, \forall x, \, f(x+p) = f(x)] \wedge f$ is not constant.

....

Proof. For contradiction assume the negation of (1). Now

$$f \text{ is not constant iff } \exists x \exists y, \; f(x) \neq f(y).$$

Thus there exists an x and y such that

$$f(x) \neq f(y).$$

Now

$$x = y \rightarrow f(x) = f(y)$$

is always true for functions. By contrapositive it follows that

$$f(x) \neq f(y) \rightarrow x \neq y.$$

Therefore, since $x \neq y$,

$$x < y \text{ or } y > x$$

CASE 1) $x < y$.

Then by P1 there exists a $p' > o$ such that

$$x + p' = y.$$

So

$$f(x + p') = f(y).$$

But since $p' > 0$, by the negation of (2) it follows that

$$f(x + p') = f(x)$$

Hence $f(x) = f(y)$.

EXERCISE

What is the contradiction? ________________________________

ANSWER:

$f(x) = f(y) \wedge f(x) \neq f(y)$

....

Note that the contradiction was deduced from the negation of (1).

CASE 2) $y < x$

Similar to CASE 1.

Since we deduced a condtradiction in both cases we have proved (1). That is, from the negated sentence we deduced an "or" sentence and from it we deduced a contradiction. ●

EXERCISES

Prove each of the following by contradiction. At the outset translate each sentence and negate it. Note carefully the deduced contradiction.

1. The product of a nonzero rational number and an irrational number is irrational.
2. For every two subsets A and B of U,

$$A \cup B \neq \emptyset \rightarrow (A \neq \emptyset \vee B \neq \emptyset)$$

3. For every subset A of U,

$$A \neq \complement A.$$

Hint: $U \neq \emptyset$ and $\complement U = \emptyset$.

4. Prove: $\sqrt{2}$ is irrational. The proof occurs in many textbooks. Feel free to consult them.

5. Prove: $\sqrt{p}$, p prime, is irrational. Hint: The proof is analogous to that of Exercise 4.

6. Prove: $\sqrt[3]{2}$ is irrational.
7. $(x \neq 0 \wedge y \neq 0) \rightarrow xy \neq 0$
8. $x > 0 \rightarrow x^{-1} > 0$
9. $x < 0 \rightarrow x^{-1} < 0$
10. For every two subsets A and B of U,

$$A \cap B \neq \emptyset \rightarrow A \neq \emptyset$$

11. For every $x > 0$,

$$\sqrt{x} < \sqrt{x+1}$$

Hint: Use the fact that for every x, $x < x + 1$.

12. For every $x > 0$,

$$x + x^{-1} \geq 2.$$

13. a) There exists an irrational number a and an irrational number b such that,

$$a^b \text{ is irrational}$$

b) Does this proof by contradiction actually exhibit an a and b such that a^b is irrational?

14. In the system of real numbers the sentence

$\forall x,\ x + 0 = 0 + x = x$

is true. Suppose there is another real number k such that

$k \neq 0$ and $\forall x,\ x + k = k + x = x$.

Deduce a contradiction.

15. In the system of real numbers the sentence

$\forall x,\ x \cdot 1 = 1 \circ x = x$

is true. Suppose there is another real number k such that

$k \neq 1$ and $\forall x,\ x \circ k = k \cdot x = x$.

Deduce a contradiction.

ANSWERS:

1. ANALYSIS: Analogous to an Example.
2. Assume for contradiction

$\exists A \exists B[\ A \cup B \neq \emptyset \wedge (A = \emptyset \wedge B = \emptyset)\ ]$

Then $(A = \emptyset \wedge B = \emptyset) \rightarrow A \cup B = \emptyset \cup B$, by substitution
$= B$
$= \emptyset$

Hence $A \cup B = \emptyset \wedge A \cup B \neq \emptyset$, a contradiction.

3. Assume for contradiction

$\exists A(A = \complement A)$

Then $A \cup \complement A = U$, by a previous exercise
$A \cup \complement A = A \cup A$, since $A = \complement A$
$= A$, by a previous exercise
Therefore $U = A$.

Also, $A \cap \complement A = \emptyset$, by a previous exercise
$A \cap \complement A = A \cap A$, since $A = \complement A$
$= A$, by a previous exercise
Therefore $\emptyset = A$.

Hence $U = \emptyset$, because $\emptyset = A$ and $U = A$. But $U \neq \emptyset$ by Axiom 4 for sets.

7. Assume for contradiction

$x \neq 0 \wedge y \neq 0 \wedge xy = 0.$

Then $x^{-1} \cdot (xy) = (x^{-1} \cdot x)y = 1 \cdot y = y$, by M4, M5. Also, since $xy=0$, $x^{-1} \circ (xy) = x^{-1} \circ 0 = 0$. Therefore $y = 0$. But $y \neq 0$ is assumed.

8. Assume for contradiction

$x > 0 \wedge x^{-1} \leq 0.$

Then $x \circ x^{-1} \leq x \cdot 0$, by 03. But $x \cdot x^{-1} = 1$ and $x \circ 0 = 0$. Therefore $1 \leq 0$. But by 07, $1 > 0$.

10. Assume for contradiction.

$\exists A \exists B(A \cap B \neq \emptyset \wedge A = \emptyset)$.

Then $A = \emptyset \rightarrow A \cap B = \emptyset \cap B = \emptyset$. Hence $A \cap B \neq \emptyset \wedge A \cap B = \emptyset$. Notice that this could also have been proved by contrapositive.

11. Assume for contradiction

$\exists x > 0, \sqrt{x} \geq \sqrt{x+1}$

Then $x = \sqrt{x} \cdot \sqrt{x} \geq \sqrt{x} \cdot \sqrt{x+1}$, by 03 since $\sqrt{x} > 0$

$\geq \sqrt{x+1} \cdot \sqrt{x+1}$, by assumption

$= x + 1$

Therefore $x \geq x + 1$, which contradicts the hint.

13. a) Hint: Having negated the sentence use the fact that $\sqrt{2}$ is irrational and consider $a = (\sqrt{2})^{\sqrt{2}}$ and $b = \sqrt{2}$.

b) No

15. Since for every real number x

$x + k = k + x = x$

then

$0 + k = k + 0 = 0$.

But we also know that $k + 0 = k$. Therefore $k = 0$. Hence $k \neq 0$ and $k = 0$, which is a contradiction.

....

PROOFS OF EXISTENCE AND UNIQUENESS

The sentence

There exists an x such that P(x)

is symbolized

$\exists x\, P(x)$.

The sentence

There exists exactly one x such that P(x)

is symbolized

$\exists !\, x\, P(x)$

Other sentences which have the same meaning as (2) are

There exists a unique x such that P(x)
There exists at least one x such that P(x), and there exists at most one x such that P(x)
There exists one and only one x such that P(x)

EXERCISES

Translate the following to logical symbolism.

1. There is a unique line ℓ such that $P \in \ell$ and $Q \in \ell$.
2. There is exactly one line containing points P and Q.
3. There is exactly one x such that for every y, $x + y = y + x = y$.
4. There is one and only one x such that for every y, $x \cdot y = y \cdot x = y$.
5. For every x and every y there is a unique z such that $x + y = z$.
6. For every x there is a unique y such that $x + y = y + x = 0$.
7. For every x there is a unique y such that if $x \neq 0$, then $x \cdot y = 1$.

ANSWERS:

1. $\exists ! \ell, P \in \ell \wedge Q \in \ell$
2. Same as 1
3. $\exists ! x \forall y, x + y = y + x = y$
4. $\exists ! x \forall y, x \cdot y = y \cdot x = y$
5. $\forall x \forall y \exists ! z, x + y = z$
6. $\forall x \exists ! y, x + y = y + x = 0$
7. $\forall x \exists ! y, x \neq 0 \rightarrow x \cdot y = 1$

. . . .

Proving Sentences of the Type $\exists ! x\, P(x)$. There are two parts to a proof of

$\exists ! x\, P(x)$.

a) Existence Part. Proving

$\exists x\, P(x)$

that is, prove there is an x such that P(x) is true.

b) Uniqueness Part. Here we must prove that if there are two elements x and z such that

P(x) is true and P(z) is true

then they must be equal. Thus, we must prove

$\forall x \forall z, [P(x) \wedge P(z)] \rightarrow x = z.$

EXAMPLE. Prove the sentence

There is a unique x such that for every y, $x + y = y + x = y$

in the real number system. Translating to logical symbolism we see that we must prove

$\exists ! x \forall y, x + y = y + x = y$

Proof.

a) Existence Part. Prove

$\exists x\, P(x)$

where P(x) is $\forall y, x + y = y + x$. Since

$\forall y,\ 0 + y = y + 0 = y$

we know that 0 is such an x.

b) Uniqueness Part. Prove

$\forall x \forall z,\ [P(x) \wedge P(z)] \rightarrow x = z$

Let x and z be arbitrary and assume $P(x) \wedge P(z)$ true. Then

$\forall y,\ x + y = y + x = y$

and

$\forall y,\ z + y = y + z = y.$

Hence

$x + z = z + x = z$

and

$z + x = x + z = x.$

Therefore

$x = z.$ ●

EXERCISES

Prove:

1. There is exactly one x such that for every y, $x \cdot y = y \cdot x = y$.
2. For every x there is a unique y such that $x + y = y + x = 0$.
3. For every x there is a unique y such that if $x \neq 0$, then $x \cdot y = y \circ x = 1$.

ANSWERS:

1. Analogous to the example.
2. Existence: See A4 of the Appendix.
   Uniqueness: Let x be arbitrary. Assume there are two elements z and y such that

   $x + y = y + x = 0$ and $x + z = z + x = 0$

   Then

   $(y + x) + z = z$, since $0 + z = z$

   $y + (x + z) = z$, associative law A2

   $y + 0 = z$, since $x + z = 0$

   $y = z$, since $y + 0 = y$

. . . .

It is time for another test. Do the following:

1) Review all material covered since the last test, but also review sentence negations.

2) Know all the modes of proof studied; that is you should know modes of proof for a given sentence.

3) Review the proofs given in the examples and exercises. Some proofs will be included on the test.

4) Allow plenty of time, perhaps a week, to study before taking the test.

Take the test only after a careful review. The purpose of the test is to decide if you have learned the previous material sufficiently to proceed with more deductively oriented mathematics courses. If you are studying this material as part of a course given by an instructor, the test will evaluate your learning and assist you in preparing for a possible classroom test.

Having completed your preparation, turn to the next page and take the test. Do not refer to the text or to your notes. You should be able to complete the test in one hour, but take all the time you need. Having completed the test, use the answer key and carry out the analysis on the page entitled "Test 2-Analysis".

TEST 2

1. A negation of

   "For every x, $x \geq 0$ or x is rational"

   is

   a) There exists an x such that $x \geq 0$ and x is rational.
   b) For every x, $x < 0$ and x is irrational.
   c) There exists an x such that $x \geq 0$ and x is irrational.
   d) There exists an x such that $x < 0$ implies that x is irrational.
   e) There exists an x such that $x < 0$ and x is irrational.

2. A negation of

   "For every e there exists a d such that if $x < d$, then $f(x) < e$"

   is

   a) There exists an e such that for every d, if $f(x) \geq e$, then $x \geq d$.
   b) For every e there exists a d such that $x < d$ and $f(x) \geq e$.
   c) There exists an e such that for every d, $x < d$ and $f(x) \geq e$.
   d) There exists an e such that for every d, if $x < d$ and $f(x) \geq e$.
   e) For every e there exists a d such that if $x < d$, then $f(x) \geq e$.

3. A mathematician gives an intricate proof of

   "x is even is a necessary condition for f to be continuous."

   He then gives an intricate proof of

   "x is odd is a sufficient condition for f to be discontinuous."

   Can you criticize what he has done? If so, how?

4. Briefly describe three different modes of proof for a sentence of the type

   "If P, then Q"

   a)

   b)

   c)

5. Briefly describe two different modes of proof for a sentence of the type

   "P if and only if Q"

a)

b)

6. Briefly describe a mode of proof for a sentence of the type

"For every x, P(x)"

7. Briefly describe <u>two</u> different modes of proof for a sentence of the type

"For every natural number n, P(n)"

a)

b)

8. Briefly describe a mode of proof for a sentence of the type

"There is some x such that P(x)"

9. Suppose you are to prove a sentence of the type

"If P or Q, then R".

List the steps you might use in the proof.

10. a) Suppose you are to give a proof by contradiction of a sentence P. Explain the steps in such a proof.

b) Suppose you are to give a proof by contradiction of a sentence

"If P, then Q".

Explain the steps in such a proof.

11. Suppose you are to prove a sentence of the type

"For every natural number n, P(n)"

by mathematical induction. List the steps in such a proof.

12. <u>Prove:</u> For every two subsets A and B of universal set U, if $A \subset B$, then $\complement B \subset \complement A$.

<u>Proof:</u>

13. Prove: If x is rational and y is irrational, then $y - x$ is irrational.

Proof.

14. Prove: For every natural number n,

$$D^n(xe^{-x}) = (-1)^n(x - n)e^{-x}$$

Proof.

15. Prove: For every two subsets A and B of universal set U,

$$\complement[A \cap \complement B] = \complement A \cup B.$$

Use any previous theorem.

Proof.

16. Prove: If x is an integer, then $x^2 + x$ is an even integer.

Proof.

KEY: (6 pts. each)

1. (6 pts.) e 2. (6 pts.) c
3. (6 pts.) The second sentence is the contrapositive of the first. Since the two sentences are equivalent, the second proof is unnecessary.
4. (2 pts. each) Any three of the following:
   a) By RCP: Assume P, deduce Q.
   b) By contrapositive: prove $\sim Q \to \sim P$.
   c) By cases: determine an intermediary step $P_1 \vee \ldots \vee P_n$ and prove

$$P \to [P_1 \vee \ldots \vee P_n] \to Q.$$

   d) By contradiction: assume $P \wedge \sim Q$ and deduce a contradiction $R \wedge \sim R$.
5. (3 pts. each) Any two of the following:
   a) Prove $P \to Q$ and $Q \to P$
   b) Prove $P \to Q$ and $\sim P \to \sim Q$
   c) By Iff-string:

$$\begin{aligned} P &\leftrightarrow Q_1 \\ &\vdots \\ &\leftrightarrow Q \end{aligned}$$

6. a) Let x be an arbitrary element of the universal set. Prove P(x) is true
   b) By contradiction
7. (3 pts. each) Any two of the following
   a) Let n be an arbitrary natural number. Prove P(n) is true.
   b) By mathematical induction
   c) By contradiction
8. a) Show or prove these exists an x in the universal set for which P(x) is true.
   b) By contradiction
9. Prove: $P \to R$ and $Q \to R$
10. a) Assume $\sim P$. Derive a contradiction of the type $R \wedge \sim R$.
    b) Assume $P \wedge \sim Q$. Derive a contradiction of the type $R \wedge \sim R$.
11. Prove

$$P(1)$$

and

$$\forall k[P(k) \to P(k+1)]$$

12. $A \subset B$ iff $\forall x,\ x \in A \to x \in B$
    iff $\forall x,\ x \notin B \to x \notin A$, by contrapositive
    iff $\forall x,\ x \in \complement B \to x \in \complement A$
    iff $\complement B \subset \complement A$
13. For contradiction, assume

x is rational,
y is irrational,

and

$y - x$ is rational.

Then

$x = \frac{a}{b}$, for some integers a and b,

and

$y - x = \frac{c}{d}$, for some integers c and d.

Thus

$$(y - x) + x = \frac{a}{b} + \frac{c}{d} = \frac{ad + bc}{bd}$$

or

$$y = \frac{ad + bc}{bd} .$$

Therefore y is rational and we have a contradiction.

14. By mathematical induction.

BASIS STEP. Prove

$$D(xe^{-x}) = (-1)(x - 1)e^{-x}$$

Now

$$D(xe^{-x}) = e^{-x} + xe^{-x} \cdot (-1)$$
$$= (-1)(x - 1)e^{-x}$$

INDUCTION STEP.

Assume: $D^k(xe^{-x}) = (-1)^k(x-1)e^{-x}$

Prove: $D^{k+1}(xe^{-x}) = (-1)^{k+1}(x-1)e^{-x}$

Now

$$D^{k+1}(xe^{-x}) = D[\, D^k(xe^{-x})\,]$$
$$= D[\, (-1)^k(x-1)e^{-x}]$$
$$= (-1)^k e^{-x} + (-1)^k(x-1)e^{-x}(-1)$$
$$= (-1)^{k+1}(x-1)e^{-x}$$

15. $\complement [A \cap \complement B] = \complement A \cup \complement\complement B$, by Theorem 8 on set theory.
$= \complement A \cup B$, by Theorem 5 on set theory.

16. Assume x is an integer. Then x is even or x is odd.

CASE 1) x is even. Then $x = 2k$ for some integer k. Therefore $x^2 = 4k^2$ and

$x^2 + x = 4k^2 + 2k = 2(2k^2 + k)$,

so $x^2 + x$ is even.

CASE 2) x is odd. Then $x = 2k + 1$ for some integer k. Therefore $x^2 = 4k^2 + 4k + 1$ and

$$\begin{aligned} x^2 + x &= 4k^2 + 6k + 2 \\ &= 2(2k^2 + 3k + 1) \end{aligned}$$

so

$x^2 + x$ is even.

TEST 2 - ANALYSIS

The test key shows the number of points for each question. Add the total you missed and subtract from 100. Review each item you missed. A score of 70 or above would be considered passing. If you scored below 70, go back in the text and review the topics pertaining to the missed items.

APPENDIX

THE REAL NUMBER SYSTEM

R denotes the real number system. R is equipped with an algrebraic structure, some properties of which are listed below. When a property also holds for the set of natural numbers N, the set of integers I, or the set of rationals Q we list the appropriate symbol to the right.

ADDITION.

A1) (Closure) $\forall a \forall b (a+b \in R)$	N, I, Q
A2) (Associative Law) $\forall a \forall b \forall c [a+(b+c)=(a+b)+c]$	N, I, Q
A3) (Additive Identity) There exists an element denoted 0, such that for every a, $a+0 = 0+a = a$.	I, Q
A4) (Additive Inverse) $\forall a \exists (-a) [a + (-a) = (-a) + a = 0]$	I, Q
A5) (Commutative Law) $\forall a \forall b (a+b = b+a)$	N, I, Q

MULTIPLICATION.

M1) (Closure) $\forall a \forall b (ab \in R)$	N, I, Q
M2) (Associative Law) $\forall a \forall b \forall c [a(bc) = (ab)c]$	N, I, Q
M3) (Multiplicative Identity) There exists an element, denoted 1, such that $\forall a (a \cdot 1 = 1 \cdot a = a)$	N, I, Q
M4) (Multiplicative Inverse) $\forall a [a \neq 0 \rightarrow \exists a^{-1} (a \cdot a^{-1} = a^{-1} \cdot a = 1)]$	Q
M5) (Commutative Law) $\forall a \forall b (ab = ba)$	N, I, Q
D) (Distributive Law) $\forall a \forall b \forall c [a(b+c)=ab + ac]$	N, I, Q
E) $1 \neq 0$	N, I, Q

ORDER PROPERTIES

01) (Trichotomy Law) For any two real numbers a, b exactly one of the following is true:

a) $a < b$, b) $a = b$, c) $a > b$ — N, I, Q

For example, $a \neq 0 \rightarrow a < 0 \vee a > 0$

02) (Transitive Law)

$\forall a \forall b \forall c[(a < b \wedge b < c) \rightarrow a < c]$ N, I, Q

03) $\forall a \forall b \forall c(a < b \rightarrow a+c < b+c)$ N, I, Q

$\forall a \forall b \forall c(a \leq b \rightarrow a+c \leq b+c)$ N, I, Q

04) $\forall a \forall b \forall c(a < b \wedge c > 0 \rightarrow ac < bc)$ N, I, Q

$\forall a \forall b \forall c(a \leq b \wedge c > 0 \rightarrow ac \leq bc)$ N, I, Q

05) $\forall a \forall b \forall c(a < b \wedge c < 0 \rightarrow ac > bc)$ N, I, Q

$\forall a \forall b \forall c(a \leq b \wedge c < 0 \rightarrow ac \geq bc)$ N, I, Q

06) $1 > 0$ N, I, Q

OTHER PROPERTIES

P1) $\forall a \forall b[a < b \leftrightarrow \exists p > 0(a+p = b)]$ N, I, Q

P2) <u>Definition.</u> $\forall a[(a \geq 0 \rightarrow |a| = a) \wedge (a < 0 \rightarrow |a| = -a)$;

then $\forall a(a \neq 0 \rightarrow |a| > 0)$ N, I, Q

P3) $\forall a(a \cdot 0 = 0 \cdot a = 0)$ I, Q

BIBLIOGRAPHY

Dodge, C. W., Sets, Logic and Numbers. Boston: Prindle, Weber and Schmidt, Inc., 1969.

Exner, R. M., and M. F. Rosskopf, Logic in Elementary Mathematics. New York: McGraw-Hill Book Co. Inc., 1959.

Hadamard, J., Psychology of Invention in the Mathematical Field. Princeton, N.J.: Princton University Press, 1945.

Keedy, M. L., A Modern Introduction to Basic Mathematics, 2nd ed. Reading, Mass: Addison-Wesley Pub. Co., 1969.

Lightstone, A. H., Symbolic Logic and the Real Number System. New York: Harper & Row, Pub., 1965.

Margaris, A., First Order Mathematical Logic. Waltham, Mass: Blaisdell Pub. Co., 1967.

Mendelson, E., Introduction to Mathematical Logic. Princeton, N.J.: D. Van Nostrand Co. Inc., 1964.

Olmsted, J. M. H., The Real Number System. New York: Appleton-Century-Crofts, 1962.

Polya, G., How to Solve It, 2nd ed. Garden City, N.Y.: Doubleday & Co., Inc., 1957.

Stoll, R. S., Set Theory and Logic. San Franciso: W. H. Freeman & Co., 1963.

INDEX

BCDE7987654321